ALSO BY PHILIP FREEMAN

St. Patrick of Ireland: A Biography

War, Women, and Druids:
Eyewitness Reports and Early Accounts of the Ancient Celts

The Galatian Language:
A Comprehensive Survey of the Language of the Ancient Celts in
Greco-Roman Asia Minor

Ireland and the Classical World

PHILIP FREEMAN

 THE

PHILOSOPHER

AND

THE DRUIDS

A
JOURNEY
AMONG
THE
ANCIENT
CELTS

Simon & Schuster
New York   London
Toronto   Sydney

SIMON & SCHUSTER
Rockefeller Center
1230 Avenue of the Americas
New York, NY 10020
Copyright © 2006 by Philip Freeman
All rights reserved,
including the right of reproduction
in whole or in part in any form.
SIMON & SCHUSTER and colophon are registered trademarks
of Simon & Schuster, Inc.
For information about special discounts for bulk purchases,
please contact Simon & Schuster Special Sales:
1-800-456-6798 or business@simonandschuster.com
Designed by Karolina Harris
Manufactured in the United States of America
10 9 8 7 6 5 4 3 2 1
Library of Congress Cataloging-in-Publication Data
Freeman, Philip, 1961–
The philosopher and the Druids : a journey among the ancient Celts / Philip Freeman.
p. cm.
Includes bibliographical references (p.) and index.
1. Civilization, Celtic. 2. Posidonius—Travel—Europe. 3. Europe—Description and
travel. 4. Europe—History—To 476. I. Title.
D70.F73 2006
913.604'3—dc22
2005054150
ISBN-13: 978-0-7432-6280-4
ISBN-10:   0-7432-6280-8

ACKNOWLEDGMENTS

I'M DEEPLY GRATEFUL to those who made this book possible—especially the teachers who introduced me to the world of Posidonius. I first heard this philosopher's name many years ago when I was an undergraduate and had the pleasure of studying Greek civilization under Professor Peter Green. While I was a graduate student, Professor John Koch pointed me toward the scattered passages of Posidonius as an amazing source of early Celtic history. Many others since then have aided me immeasurably in my own explorations of the Celts in the classical world— I offer special thanks to Barry Cunliffe, Joseph Eska, Patrick Ford, James Mallory, Gregory Nagy, Joseph Nagy, and Christopher Snyder.

I was honored to be selected as a Visiting Scholar at the Harvard Divinity School during 2004–5, which provided an unparalleled setting and resources for research. My home institution of Luther College in beautiful Decorah, Iowa, was gracious in allowing me to take advantage of this wonderful opportunity.

Joëlle Delbourgo, Bob Bender, and Johanna Li all patiently led me through the publication process. But my greatest thanks are to my wife, Alison, who makes all things possible.

CONTENTS

LIST OF ILLUSTRATIONS

IRELAND

BRITAIN

GERMANY

Atlantic

Ocean

Hochdorf

Danube

Vix

La Tène

Alps

Hallsta

GAUL

LEPONTII

CISALPINE
GAUL

Mediolanum

Po R.

Rhone R.

LIGURIA

Adria

*Pyrenees
mountains*

Massalia

ETRURIA

Telamon

Clusium

LUSITANIA

Numantia

Ebro R.

CELTIBERIA

Rome

ITAL

SPAIN

Balearic Islands

SARDINIA

Guadalquivir R.

Tartessus

Cádiz

Mediterranean Sea

Pillars of Hercules

Carthage

SICIL

AFRICA

| 0 Miles | 200 | 400 |
| 0 Kilometers | 400 | |

© 2005 Jeffrey L. Ward

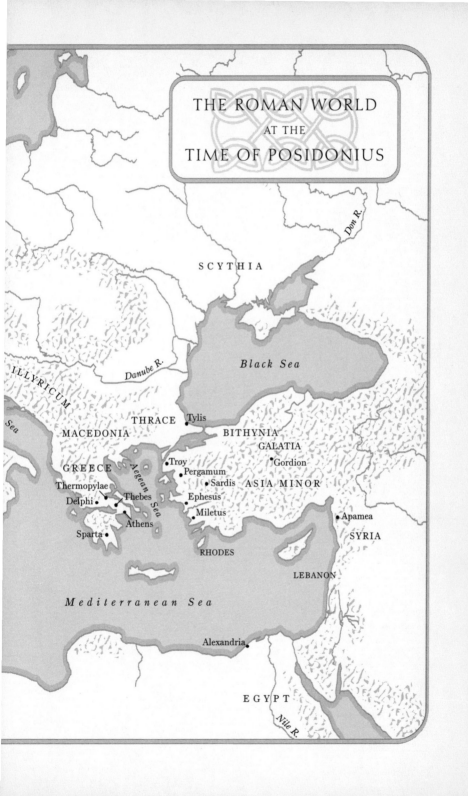

THE ROMAN WORLD
AT THE
TIME OF POSIDONIUS

Don R.

SCYTHIA

Danube R.

Black Sea

ILLYRICUM

Sea

THRACE • Tylis

MACEDONIA

BITHYNIA

GALATIA

• Gordion

GREECE

• Troy
• Pergamum

Aegean Sea

• Sardis   ASIA MINOR

Thermopylae

Ephesus

Delphi •   • Thebes

• Miletus

• Apamea

Athens

SYRIA

Sparta •

RHODES

LEBANON

Mediterranean Sea

• Alexandria

EGYPT

Nile R.

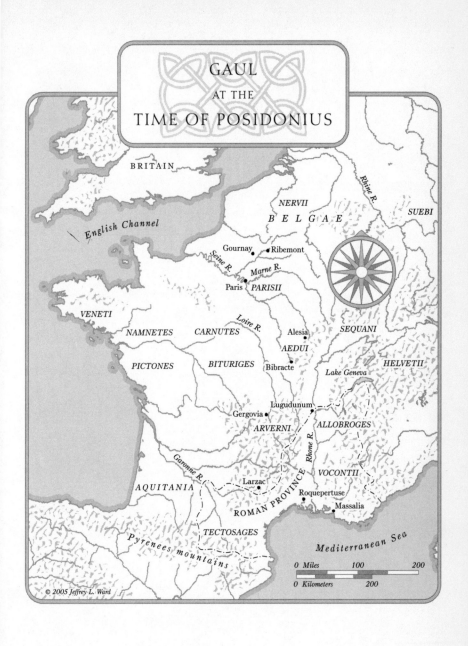

GAUL

AT THE

TIME OF POSIDONIUS

BRITAIN

English Channel

NERVII

B E L G A E

SUEBI

Rhine R.

Seine R.

Gournay • • Ribemont

Marne R.

Paris • *PARISII*

VENETI

Loire R.

NAMNETES   CARNUTES

Alesia •

SEQUANI

AEDUI

PICTONES   BITURIGES

Bibracte •

Lake Geneva

HELVETII

Lugudunum •

Gergovia •

ARVERNI

ALLOBROGES

Garonne R.

Rhone R.

AQUITANIA

Larzac •

VOCONTII

Roquepertuse •

ROMAN PROVINCE

Massalia •

TECTOSAGES

Mediterranean Sea

Pyrenees mountains

0 Miles   100   200

0 Kilometers   200

© 2005 Jeffrey L. Ward

THE
PHILOSOPHER
AND
THE DRUIDS

INTRODUCTION

"Celtic" . . . is a magic bag, into which anything may be put,
and out of which almost anything may come. . . . Anything is
possible in the fabulous Celtic twilight.

J. R. R. TOLKIEN

ONE WARM SUMMER DAY in the year 335 B.C., a young
Alexander the Great was sitting outside his tent on the banks of
the Danube River. His father, Philip of Macedon, had been
murdered just the year before during a wedding, but Alexander
had lost no time in seizing his father's throne and firmly estab-
lishing his own rule throughout Macedonia and Greece. Philip
had long nursed a dream of invading the mighty Persian Empire to the east, a vast kingdom stretching from the borders of
Greece to Syria, Egypt, Babylon, and all the way to India.
Alexander shared this vision and prepared for the upcoming
Persian campaign by securing his northern frontiers against the
wild tribes of Thracians and Scythians who rode south to raid
and pillage whenever they saw an opportunity.

Alexander had just defeated these fearsome warriors of the
north in battle using the legendary daring and determination
that would soon gain him the largest empire the world had ever
known. But on this day the twenty-one-year-old Macedonian
general and former student of the philosopher Aristotle was
content to rest from war and enjoy the glow of victory with his
companions. Among them was a young man named Ptolemy, a
childhood friend of Alexander who now served as a trusted lieutenant. Twelve years later, after Alexander's death, Ptolemy
would seize control of Egypt and establish a ruling dynasty that
would end with his descendant Cleopatra.

Ptolemy's memoir records that as Alexander sat before his tent, a small group of warriors approached the camp and asked for an audience with the king. They were unusually tall men with drooping mustaches, each wearing a gleaming gold torque—a sort of thick necklace—around his neck, and a brightly colored tunic that reached halfway to his knees. They carried long swords in finely decorated scabbards attached to chain belts, while flowing cloaks of checkerboard green were fastened around their shoulders with enormous gold brooches. Strangest indeed to the eyes of a civilized Greek was the utterly barbaric way they dressed below the waist— they wore, of all things, pants.

The embassy approached the astonished King and presented themselves as Celts who had traveled from the mountains of the west to seal a pact of goodwill with the victorious monarch. Alexander welcomed them warmly, assured them of his peaceful intentions toward their people, and invited them to share a drink of fine Greek wine. The Celts gladly accepted, though they refused an offer to dilute the wine with water as was the Mediterranean custom. Aristotle had taught Alexander never to pass up an opportunity to discover something new about the world, so the young general eagerly inquired about Celtic culture, history, and religion. Finally, when their tongues were thoroughly loosened by drink, Alexander asked his visitors one last question: *What do you fear the most?* Most men in such a situation would naturally have turned to flattery and quickly answered that they most feared the military might of the great general who sat across from them. But the leader of the Celtic band soberly looked Alexander in the eye and said, "Nothing. We honor the friendship of a man like you more than anything in the world, but we are afraid of nothing at all. Except," he added with a grin, "that the sky might fall down on our heads!" The rest of the Celtic warriors laughed along with their leader as they rose and bade farewell to the Macedonians. Alexander watched them stride out of camp and begin the long trek back to their mountain home. He then turned to his friends and exclaimed, "What braggarts these Celts are!"

This meeting between Alexander and the Celts was one of the earliest encounters between the Greeks and an almost legendary people who lived in the unexplored forests and mountains of western Europe. The few Greek records of the Celts before Alexander's time speak only of a wild and uncivilized collection of tribes known as the *Keltoi,* who dwelled in the distant lands of Italy, Spain, and beyond the Alps, all the way to the mysterious northern sea. But the Celts were rapidly becoming a force in the classical world. In the decades before Alexander, they had swept south over the alpine passes and breached the gates of Rome. Fifty years after Alexander, they would attack the sacred Greek site of Delphi, home to Apollo's oracle, and cross the Hellespont into Asia Minor, ravaging the coast before settling permanently in their own kingdom of Galatia in the middle of the Greek world. From that time to the end of the Roman Republic, the Celts would be a constant threat to the civilized lands of the Mediterranean. Only with the crushing defeat of the Gauls by Julius Caesar in the first century B.C. would the Celts virtually disappear from the stage of history.

TODAY, more than two thousand years after Caesar, the Celts are everywhere. Turn on the radio and you can hear the lilting melodies of Celtic music. Browse your local bookstore and count the numerous volumes available on Celtic art, history, mythology, and spirituality. Hollywood movies regularly feature fearless Celtic warriors facing down a vastly superior enemy or immortal elves speaking a hauntingly beautiful language of Celtic origin. You can watch high-stepping Celtic dance at almost any local folk festival or purchase intricately crafted Celtic jewelry.

But who were the Celts? Do modern ideas of Celtic culture have genuine roots stretching back to ancient times? If so, what were these Celts of Greek and Roman times really like?

The truth about the Celts may surprise you, because many of the most common ideas about them are based on fantasy or, at best, half-truths. They were not wild and mindless barbarians who knew little of civilized ways but a sophisticated and technologically advanced culture spread throughout Europe who in many ways surpassed the Greeks and Romans. Did the priests of the Celts, the Druids, really practice human sacrifice? Yes—archaeology and ancient literary sources firmly agree that they did, but they were also believers in reincarnation who studied the subtle movement of the stars and composed hauntingly beautiful poetry. Were women really equal to men in ancient Celtic society? Yes and no—it was definitely a man's world, but a Celtic woman had rights and power even Cleopatra might have envied.

We know about the ancient Celts through different kinds of evidence, such as Greek and Roman writers, archaeology, and the emerging study of early Celtic languages. But by far our best source for the true story of the Celts comes from the pen of a single man who is scarcely remembered today—a Greek philosopher of the first century B.C. named Posidonius. When Posidonius was a young man, he set out on an extraordinary journey to the still unconquered Celtic lands of western Europe. Rome was even then beginning to sweep into Celtic territory. It was only a matter of time before the unstoppable legions would move north and destroy what remained of independent Celtic life in continental Europe. But Posidonius was a scientist as well as a philosopher, a man skilled at careful observation and methodical record keeping. Just as Lewis and Clark journeyed to discover the American West and its native people before both were changed forever, Posidonius set out on a mission to uncover the truth about the Celts before they were swallowed up by Rome.

The account Posidonius wrote of his journey was his *History,* a marvel of ethnic study that became a best-seller across the Mediterranean world. But somehow in early Christian times it disappeared, so that not a single copy of this priceless book survives today. However, we can reconstruct much of the lost original by carefully sifting through ancient authors, both famous and obscure, and piecing together like a jigsaw puzzle the scattered fragments of Posidonius that they quote. Even though many parts of the puzzle are forever lost, enough remain to create a vivid picture of a vanished people. By building on this forgotten *History* of Posidonius, along with the works of other early writers and recent discoveries by archaeologists, we can uncover the fascinating and true story of the ancient Celts.

ONE

POSIDONIUS

Posidonius—a native of Apamea in Syria and citizen of Rhodes. He was a
Stoic philosopher whose nickname was "the Athlete."
BYZANTINE *SUDA* ENCYCLOPEDIA

POSIDONIUS was born about the year 135 B.C. in Syria, far from the land of the Celts. Syria may seem like a strange birthplace for a man who would become one of the best-known Greek philosophers of ancient times, but given his topsy-turvy world, it makes perfect sense. Posidonius lived in a world between two ages—the glory days of Athenian democracy, the Olympic games, and the artistic achievements of fifth-century B.C. Greece were all long past or just shadows of their former selves. There was still remarkable creativity and energy in the second century B.C., but it was as if everyone was holding his breath and waiting. In the Mediterranean world of young Posidonius, all eyes were turned west, toward the rising power of Rome.

TO UNDERSTAND the turbulent life and times of Posidonius—and his subsequent journey among the Celts—we have to look deep into Greek history. Two thousand years before Posidonius, a loosely organized and fearlessly independent group of tribes later known as the Hellenes or Greeks moved southward from their ancestral home on the steppes of the Ukraine into the mountains of Greece. The Greek tribes had sprung from a common cultural and linguistic group called the Indo-Europeans, which also gave rise to the Romans, Germans, Armenians, Scythians, Persians, and inhabitants of northern

India, among many other groups, including the ancestors of the Celts. The Indo-Europeans were masters of warfare who worshiped a host of constantly quarreling divinities led by a paternal sky god, known later among the Greeks as Zeus and the Romans as Jupiter.

The mountainous terrain of Greece was totally unlike the northern plains of the Indo-European homeland, so the Greeks soon settled into a scattered collection of separate kingdoms connected more often by sea than by land. Under the influence of the Egyptians, Minoans, and the ancient civilizations of the Near East, they grew into a wealthy and powerful culture known as the Mycenaeans, with trade connections stretching far to the west and east. One trading partner and sometimes rival of the Mycenaean Greeks was the famed kingdom of Troy in modern Turkey, which controlled the entrance to the Black Sea. Sometime around 1200 B.C., Troy was sacked by invaders who may well have been Greeks bent on riches and glory. Whether Homer's later account of Achilles, Agamemnon, and the Trojan Horse is more fiction or fact is debatable, but the tale of Troy's destruction became the central myth of the Greeks for centuries to come.

Soon after the fall of Troy, the Mycenaean kingdoms of Greece themselves collapsed under outside invasions, internal turmoil, or both. Five hundred years passed in which the Greeks farmed their rocky land, sacrificed to their gods, and sang of mighty Hercules, wily Odysseus, and ill-fated Oedipus. Beginning in the eighth century B.C., the Greeks adopted writing from the Phoenicians of Lebanon and started to record their myths and poetry. At the same time began the rise of the *polis* or city-state—places such as Athens, Sparta, and Thebes, which rapidly grew in power and military might. Then, in the sixth century, the Babylonian Empire centered in modern Iraq was overthrown by the Persians, who quickly became an enormously powerful and threatening neighbor to the Greeks. In the Greek records of the time, *a* king could be from anywhere, but *the* king was Persian.

In 490 B.C., the Persian king Darius made his move into Greece. At the Battle of Marathon near Athens, in a contest many had deemed hopeless, ten thousand Greeks routed perhaps twice as many Persians and drove them back across the Aegean Sea. Ten years later, three hundred Spartans and their allies held back a second Persian invasion at the narrow pass of Thermopylae, buying time for the Athenians and other Greeks to organize a force that would defeat the Persians once and for all. From this defeat of the world's greatest empire sprang the confidence to create the Golden Age of fifth-century B.C. Greece. The Athenians built the still-standing masterpiece the Parthenon on their Acropolis as a temple to their namesake goddess, Athena. In the shadow of the Parthenon, Socrates taught philosophy and the plays of Sophocles were first performed. The contemporary Athenian leader Pericles said that later ages would marvel at the city—and we still do. But all was not well in Greece. Athenian political leadership against the Persians soon turned to brutal empire building and subjugation of fellow Greeks. Sparta and her Greek allies destroyed Athenian power in the decades-long Peloponnesian War, leaving all of Greece weak and exhausted.

It was just the opportunity the Macedonians had been waiting for. Long tired of being dismissed as semibarbarians, the Macedonians under the leadership of Alexander the Great's father, Philip, were determined to teach their haughty Greek neighbors to the south a lesson in respect. In August 338 B.C., Philip defeated the Theban army and became master of the Greek world. His dream of conquering the Persians was thwarted in 336 by an assassin's blade—reportedly Celtic in origin—but his son Alexander quickly took up his father's mantle and crossed into Persian territory soon after his encounter with the Celtic embassy at the Danube.

Alexander the Great's conquest of the Persian Empire was a military marvel. The story is told by countless ancient historians and later interpreters and is even mentioned in the great

Sundiata epic of medieval west Africa. In the wake of Alexander's troops came Greek colonists and administrators who settled from Egypt to Afghanistan. The heirs to Alexander's empire—such as Ptolemy in Egypt and Seleucus in Syria—carved Greek kingdoms from the lands of the Persians, Egyptians, Jews, Babylonians, Bactrians, and many others. Alexander had dreamed of a new world in which the best of Greek civilization and indigenous cultures harmoniously blended. Instead, the Greek colonists and dominated natives lived side by side in different worlds. The great Greek city of Alexandria at the mouth of the Nile was not a blend of Egyptian and Hellenic culture but a glaringly Greek city as psychologically distant from the land of the pharaohs as was Athens. Although there was definitely a diffusion of Greek culture and language throughout the eastern Mediterranean, northern Africa, and western Asia, it was no more enthusiastically adopted by most natives than was British culture in Victorian India. Almost alone among the Mediterranean peoples, the unconquered Romans willingly, though always with reservations, fused Greek culture with their own.

THUS Posidonius was born a Greek in the city of Apamea on the coast of Syria two hundred years after Alexander's death. Apamea was founded by Alexander's general Seleucus as a military colony for his veterans and for other Macedonian and Greek settlers. By the time of Posidonius, it was a flourishing city with thousands of inhabitants known for cosmopolitan trade, beautiful gardens, and elephant breeding. Although surrounded by speakers of Aramaic and other languages from farther east, Posidonius was Greek to the core. He came from a family of Greek settlers who would no more have thought themselves Syrian than the seventeenth-century Pilgrims of Massachusetts would have considered themselves Wampanoag Indians. Posidonius certainly expresses no love for his native land in his writing. In one fragment, he mocks the native people of Apamea heading off to an earlier war: "Clutching knives on their belts and filthy, rusting spears . . . dragging behind them donkeys piled high with all manner of wine, food, flutes, and musical instruments—prepared for a party rather than a battle."

The early education of Posidonius in Apamea would have been like that of any other Greek boy of his age and social standing. A liberal education was the very heart of Greekness and was enthusiastically encouraged in Greek colonies throughout the Hellenistic world. At about the age of seven, boys were first marched to a local school by a family slave. There they learned the basics of reading and writing, practiced gymnastics, then progressed to music, poetry, mathematics, and literature. Memorization and recitation were the rule, with every student required to learn vast amounts of Greek poetry, especially Homer, by heart. Discipline was notoriously strict—it's no coincidence that the symbol of many elementary teachers was a whipping cane.

In their early teens, students moved on to a more intense study of all subjects, such as poetry, history, philosophy, and science—though the last was always theoretical rather than experimental. But public speaking, or rhetoric, was the central feature of an education that prepared young men to take their place in the civic world. Students would learn to argue their way through different historical or imaginary situations, then switch and defend the opposite position. Physical education continued during these years in the *gymnasion*—literally "naked place"—and that may well have been where Posidonius earned his nickname of "Athlete."

ONE OF THE SUBJECTS studied by Posidonius and every other Greek boy was ethnography—the examination of non-Greeks and their native lands. The Greeks were always fascinated by foreign cultures, as long as those societies remained at a distance. By a Greek, anyone not Greek was disdainfully thought of as a *barbaros,* or barbarian—someone whose words sounded like unintelligible *bar-bar* sounds. The Greeks, like the ancient Chinese, were completely confident that their civilization was the epitome of human society. Other cultures could only strive to become what they already were.

This biased point of view begins with Homer, whose world was a small place, stretching out from Greece only as far as Italy, Egypt, and the closer parts of the Near East. But widespread Greek colonization in following centuries and the subsequent Persian Wars expanded the known world from Spain to India. The first great Greek ethnographic writer was Herodotus of Halicarnassus, in the fifth century B.C., whose history of the Persian Wars frequently wanders into marvelous digressions on tribes from the Mediterranean and beyond. His description of the relatively nearby Egyptians is typical of his technique—minimal investigation enlarged heavily by local tales and secondhand stories:

> Egyptian customs are the opposite of those of all other people. Among the Egyptians, women do the buying and selling, while men stay at home and weave. . . . Women carry heavy loads on their shoulders, but men on their heads. Women urinate standing up, though men sit. Both sexes relieve themselves indoors and eat their meals outside—for as they say, shameful things should be done out of view, but honorable things in the open.

But even in Herodotus, there are the beginnings of scientific investigation. He did at least take the trouble to visit Egypt to gather his stories, unlike Greeks before him, who simply repeated gossip derived at the local dock from sailors and merchants. However, the farther Herodotus progresses from Greece in his ethnography, the less reliable and more wild his tales become. On the northern edge of Asia, beyond even the nomadic Scythians of the modern Ukraine, he describes a people who have hooves like goats, eat their dead fathers, and sleep six months of the year. But Herodotus is quick to add that, even though he repeats such reports, he doesn't believe them.

Posidonius and his schoolmates would have read Herodotus, but it was more recent Greek historians, such as the second-century B.C. Polybius, who were on the forefront of ethnographic writing. Polybius was an aristocrat from southern Greece whose history of Rome's rise to power broke new ground in the study of distant lands and events. His techniques consisted of the careful use of reliable sources along with personal investigation. To write accurately of Hannibal's famed crossing of the Alps with war elephants, Polybius exhaustively examined firsthand records, then personally retraced the arduous path of Rome's most fearsome enemy. As Polybius himself says: "I undertook dangerous journeys through Africa, Spain, and Gaul, even sailing beyond these countries, to correct the reports of earlier historians and accurately describe these distant lands to the Greeks." In the scientific history of Polybius, the young Posidonius found a model for his own later research among the Celts.

AFTER COMPLETING secondary school, the best students, like Posidonius, would progress to the ancient equivalent of a university education at centers of higher learning around the eastern Mediterranean, such as Ephesus, Alexandria, or especially Athens, known above all else for the study of philosophy. There were advanced schools in different subjects, such as medicine and literature, but it was philosophy that most appealed to the young Greek from Syria. As Posidonius sailed into the Athenian port of Piraeus, he must have gazed in wonder at the distant Acropolis. He knew that this city of Plato and Aristotle, though long past its prime, was still the cultural heart of the Greek world. The choice now before Posidonius was which of the rival schools of philosophy he would attend.

Western philosophy began in the sixth century B.C., when Greeks living on the western coast of Asia Minor started to question the power of the Olympian gods in Greek mythology. They began an exploration of the universe that emphasized scientific rather than religious explanations, though most accepted that a divine force benignly governed the cosmos. Anaximander of Miletus said the universe consists of an underlying element he called the Infinite, which guides the constantly shifting world we see before us. Heraclitus of Ephesus urged anyone interested in *philosophia* ("the love of wisdom") to closely examine the world around them for the secrets of nature. Pythagoras of Samos—best known today for his famed geometrical theorem—was one of the most influential and mysterious of the early Greek philosophers. Pythagoras saw numerical underpinnings in all of nature and made key discoveries in music as well as mathematics. But he was also famous in the ancient world for his exotic theory of the transmigration of souls. The human spirit, he believed, is eternal and passes into other forms and bodies after death.

Socrates of Athens took up the call of philosophy in the fifth century B.C. and spent his life forcing people to question their most dearly held beliefs. He was executed in 399 B.C. for his trouble, but not before he deeply influenced men such as Plato to devote their lives to philosophy. Plato's copious fourth-century B.C. writings reveal the mind of a brilliant thinker who commented on almost every aspect of the human condition, from the ideal government to the nature of the soul. His most lasting contribution to philosophy is his theory claiming that the fundamental ideas or forms of the universe—such as truth, justice, and goodness—exist independent of humanity. Plato's practical-minded student Aristotle questioned some of these teachings but made important contributions to myriad areas of philosophy and science that exerted a powerful influence on intellectuals for centuries.

At the time of young Posidonius, Plato and Aristotle were still considered the high points of Greek philosophy, but the Hellenistic age was bursting with new philosophical paths to follow. One choice open to a student was Epicureanism, a much-maligned but popular philosophy in Greek and Roman times. Pleasure is the beginning and end of happiness, said its founder, Epicurus of Athens. Epicurus had studied Plato's philosophy but found it ultimately unsatisfying. In his thirties he bought a garden home and settled there with his followers to live a communal life built on the pursuit of pleasure. Far from the hedonistic debauchery one might expect, the Epicurean community—including slaves and women—lived an almost monastic life. Although pleasure was their goal, they believed moderation and contemplative living were the means to this end. Later Christians condemned the Epicureans not only for their focus on pleasure but also for their rejection of a caring divinity and denial of the soul's immortality—in Dante's *Inferno*, they are buried alive in scorching hot tombs—but many in the classical age admired their seemingly reasonable and idyllic way of life.

The ultimate in uncomplicated living was advocated by the Cynics (dog people), a group founded by Diogenes, who allegedly slept in a large jar and went about Athens with a lantern scornfully looking for an honest man (hence the modern term *cynical*). Diogenes and his followers earned their name by rejecting social conventions and performing all bodily functions in public, like dogs. Cynics claimed to follow a life attuned to nature, but to many ancient and modern critics they were simply self-centered rebels who refused to grow up. The original dropouts of human history, the early Cynics had little to offer as philosophers other than an austere way of life. But in time, many Cynics softened their stance and developed ideas that exerted a great influence on Greek and Roman thought.

Neither Epicureanism nor Cynicism appealed to Posidonius. Instead, he was drawn to the philosophical movement known as Stoicism. Zeno, the originator of the movement, came to Athens in the late fourth century B.C. to study philosophy and eventually founded his own school at a nearby *stoa* (porch). From the beginning, Stoicism was wide-ranging in its beliefs but always emphasized logic, an orderly universe, and a strict moral philosophy based on a pursuit of virtue and a rejection of emotions. The belief in a divine guiding principle was ever-present in Stoic thought, but this vision of God was distant from the personal notion of divinity in modern monotheistic religions. As Posidonius himself wrote: "God is an intelligent, burning breath—formless, ever-changing into what he wishes, becoming a part of everything." Stoics definitely believed in a divine being, but also central to their philosophy was faith in the power of a disciplined human being to make decisions independent of any fate or god.

The Stoic philosopher and ex-slave Epictetus in the early Christian era sums up the proper behavior for a Stoic in the beginning of his *Handbook*:

> Some things are in our control, but others are not. . . . Regarding any objects that please you, are useful, or loved, remind yourself of their true nature, starting with the smallest things in your life. If you have a favorite cup, remember that what you really like are cups in general, not any specific cup. This way, if it breaks, you won't be upset. Likewise, when you kiss your children or wife, remind yourself that what you are really kissing and love is humanity—this way you won't be troubled if your wife or child dies.

It's no coincidence that with such a rigid and unemotional philosophy, an unfeeling person even today is known as stoic. Not every follower of Stoicism would have accepted such an extreme way of life, but the movement had a huge following in Hellenistic times and later counted famous Romans such as Seneca and the emperor Marcus Aurelius as adherents.

Posidonius probably chose Stoicism not so much because of its strict ethics but because of its emphasis on reason and logic.

It was the natural choice for a young man with a scientific frame of mind. For Posidonius, the world and all that was in it was a great puzzle waiting to be solved.

POSIDONIUS studied at the Stoic school in Athens under the direction of the famed teacher Panaetius, then settled on the beautiful island of Rhodes in the Aegean Sea. Though we know few details of Posidonius's life, we can be sure that in Rhodes he was granted citizenship and founded his own school of philosophy, which was destined to draw students from not only the Greek world but Rome as well.

Sometime during these early years in Rhodes, a daring notion first entered the mind of Posidonius. He had been taught by his Stoic professors that the world and all its people were part of a divine order. What better way to understand this order than a great journey of exploration? He knew that tribes still relatively uncorrupted by civilizing influences would be an important part of such a study. To be sure, this grand excursion would be the perfect opportunity to explore other subjects—astronomy, geology, and oceanography just to name a few—as well, but it was unspoiled human culture Posidonius most wanted to examine. But where to go? To the south and east lay the ancient and long-civilized lands of Egypt and Mesopotamia. To the north were the wild Scythians, but Greeks had been living among them and writing about them since before Herodotus. The best possibility lay in the last place any reasonable Greek philosopher would want to go. In the distant west, beyond even the rule of Rome, lay the unknown land of the Celts.

TWO

BEGINNINGS

The heavens and earth are divided into four parts—the Indians occupy the
land of the east wind, the Ethiopians that of the south wind,
the Celts the west, and the Scythians the north.

EPHORUS, *ON EUROPE*

SAIL WEST from Posidonius's island home at Rhodes in the Aegean and you'll eventually come to the Adriatic Sea, between Greece and Italy. Travel north to the head of these waters, near present-day Venice, continue north, cross the snowcapped Alps rising before you, and you'll discover one of the most beautiful places on earth. Here on the shores of a stunning blue lake beneath mountains soaring to the sky lies the Austrian village of Hallstatt.

In the year 1846, Johann Georg Ramsauer was surveying the ancient salt mines above Hallstatt when he stumbled on a graveyard. In between his official duties at the mine, this young Austrian engineer began a systematic excavation of the huge burial site that lasted sixteen years. Archaeology was in its infancy at the time, with most diggers being little more than treasure hunters, but Ramsauer was no grave robber. He used his considerable technical and artistic skills to meticulously uncover and record the contents of over a thousand graves. In the burials were a rich collection of magnificent swords, intricate metalwork and pottery, and hundreds of carefully laid-out human skeletons alone or in small groups. No one had ever found anything like it in central Europe. To Ramsauer and others trained in classical history, there could be no doubt—he had discovered an early graveyard of the Celts.

Today, we know the first period of Celtic civilization simply as the Hallstatt era. Most of the artifacts found by Ramsauer date from the seventh and sixth centuries B.C.—a time of tremendous social change in continental Europe north of the Alps. And although pots and swords are mute witnesses, few scholars would doubt that if the bones Ramsauer found could talk, they would speak a Celtic tongue.

But the Celts who lived at Hallstatt in the seventh century B.C., as well as those Posidonius would meet six hundred years later in Gaul, did not simply rise fully formed from the earth. A complex and fascinating series of events took place over many centuries before the people we know today as the Celts came to power in Iron Age Europe.

TEN THOUSAND years ago, the last of the great sheets of ice that had covered northern Europe and the Alps began their rapid retreat. Sea levels rose as the glaciers melted, separating Britain from the continent and pouring an awesome flood into the Black Sea. With warmer weather, settlers quickly moved into the formerly cold lands from all directions. Farming was still many centuries away, but these earliest northern Europeans hunted abundant animals and gathered plants that sustained rich cultures from Ireland to Russia. We can do little more than guess at life in these ancient times, but as in all communities, children were born, the dead were buried, and stories of gods and heroes were passed from generation to generation.

About 7000 B.C., people living in the great river valleys of Mesopotamia, Egypt, and eastern Asia developed farming and began domesticating animals for their meat, milk, and wool. Agriculture spread rapidly westward and northward into Europe, giving rise to the first permanent settlements north of the Alps. At about the same time, the great Indo-European migrations from the steppes of Ukraine began. The ancestors of the

Germans, Greeks, Celts, and Italic peoples moved into Europe from the east. When exactly the Celts broke off as a separate group is unknown, but they seem to have been closely in touch with or even part of the same group as the ancestors of the Romans during these early centuries. Even today, when scholars look at the ancient and modern Celtic languages, they find the closest relatives for Celtic words in Latin dictionaries.

However long the ancestors of the Celts lived in close contact with the Italic people, Germans, and others, eventually they broke away to form their own unique culture in central Europe. Finding the earliest signs of the Celts, however, is a problem. Hallstatt objects date back to the seventh century B.C., but the Celts must have been in the area long before that time. One of the best candidates for these earlier Celts lies in what archaeologists call the Urnfield culture.

In about 1300 B.C., a new type of burial rite spread across central Europe; in it the cremated remains of the deceased were placed in urns, then buried in well-organized cemeteries. This culture stretched far beyond probable Celtic lands, but in the area just to the north and east of the Alps, we can see the remains of a particular branch of the Urnfield group that bears a striking resemblance to the later Hallstatt Celts. There is a strong continuity in metalwork, tools, and jewelry in this region into Hallstatt times that can mean only that the ancestors of the Celts were already present north of the Alps by the late second millennium B.C. The Urnfield period in the alpine zone seems to have been a time of relative stability and economic growth. Populations were on the rise as well, indicating an abundance of food supplies. We also start to see hill forts in this period, with the beginnings of rich burials featuring all manner of horse gear—a sure sign of an emerging warrior aristocracy.

BY THE EIGHTH CENTURY B.C., great changes were taking place across the Mediterranean world that were felt even north of the Alps. At the same time as Homer was composing his

songs of Troy, the Greeks were beginning a great age of colonization. Different Greek cities—whether for commercial gain or because of overpopulation—were founding colonies around the
Mediterranean and the Black Sea. Many of these colonists settled in Sicily and around the Bay of Naples in Italy. From there
they spread Greek goods and culture inland to the native tribes
and up the Italian peninsula to the Etruscans just north of
Rome. In about 600 B.C., colonists from the Greek city of Phocaea founded Massalia (modern Marseilles) near the mouth of
the Rhone River in southern Gaul. The trade routes spreading
north up the Rhone from Massalia were to have a tremendous
impact on the Celts, as did the more direct routes over the Alps
from the growing Etruscan cities of north-central Italy. Greeks
in time also expanded their trade all the way to southern Spain
and beyond into the Atlantic Ocean, to the kingdom of Tartessus just beyond the Strait of Gibraltar. There they met Phoenician merchants, who had preceded them many years earlier. In
Spain they saw for themselves the rich silver mines of Iberia
and learned of trade routes in tin and gold stretching north to
the mysterious islands of the Albiones and Hierni—known to
later geographers as Britain and Ireland.

But not all the influences on the Celts came from the south.
On the eastern steppes a people known to Greek historians as
the Cimmerians were on the move westward. These mighty
horsemen from the plains of southern Russia poured into what
is modern Hungary, bringing with them an ancient tradition of
beautiful decorative art filled with elaborate and stylized animal
figures. They also brought a new breed of larger, more powerful
horses that through trade soon reached the land of the Celts.
Horses had long been a feature in Urnfield culture, but this
breed brought cavalry warfare to a whole new level. No longer
were the aristocrats of the Celts content to ride their small
horses merely as transport. Now, with larger animals, they
could take their mounts directly into battle, slashing their enemies with longer swords made for use on horseback.

The combination of Greek and Etruscan luxury goods from the south and the influence of the horsemen from the eastern plains acted like a catalyst on the Urnfield ancestors of the Celts. Suddenly the modestly ornate graves of Urnfield aristocrats became showplaces of Mediterranean goods and eastern-inspired cavalry gear. Tribal leaders, who once placed the ashes of their fathers in simple urns, began instead to lay out the bodies unburned in rich tombs full of ceremonial war carts, Greek wine, elaborate furniture, gleaming iron weapons, and even silk imported from distant China. It was an age of conspicuous consumption among the new Hallstatt nobility. Whether the average Celtic farm family was pleased with or benefited greatly from this new age is an open question, but the warrior aristocracy was having a grand time.

One of the most striking examples of the new Hallstatt elite is a well-preserved grave at Hochdorf, near Stuttgart, Germany, dating to the late sixth century B.C. This grave chamber—larger than the average modern dining room—was constructed as an enormous wooden box and covered over by stone to discourage grave robbers (as with ancient Egyptian tombs, many Hallstatt graves were plundered in antiquity). Inside the tomb archaeologists found the remains of a man over six feet tall and about forty years old, covered in gold from head to foot. The torque around his neck was also gold, as were his dagger, arm ring, and belt—even his shoes were covered in gold leaf. He lay fully stretched out on a metal couch decorated with four-wheeled wagons and figures in single combat. The couch was supported by eight bronze casters of finely decorated female figures, each riding on a single wheel like a unicycle. A huge bronze caldron with carved lions sitting on the rim was positioned at the dead man's feet. Modern tests have revealed that the caldron was filled with mead at the time of the burial, strongly suggesting the warrior's family was sending him off to an eternal feast. The rest of the tomb contained drinking horns, colored embroidery, and an entire four-wheeled wooden wagon covered in iron and bronze sheeting.

But it wasn't only men who received such grandiose burials in the Hallstatt age. Near Vix in eastern France archaeologists have discovered a burial from about the same time as the Hochdorf grave but containing the body of a female. This woman—surely a high-ranked aristocrat—was sent to the afterlife with not only the standard four-wheeled wagon but also Etruscan metalwork and an enormous bronze wine jar imported from Greece in her wood-lined grave. Like most Celts from this early period all the way to medieval Irish times, she wore a decorated torque around her neck.

The Hallstatt era of Celtic history lasted until about 450 B.C., at which point there was a change in Celtic society that can be described only as a social and artistic revolution. For over two centuries the Celtic elite along the northern edge of the Alps had been building magnificent tombs, trading with the Mediterranean lands for luxury goods, and evidently lording it over their poorer Celtic cousins farther north. But in the middle of the fifth century B.C., just as Socrates was beginning his career as a professional troublemaker in Athens, the Hallstatt world came abruptly to an end. Traditional burials ceased, forts were burned to the ground, and four-wheeled vehicles all but vanished. At almost the same time, however, there was an explosion of creativity and new types of burials in the previous frontier Celtic zone farther north of the Alps.

This new era, named La Tène after an archaeological site in Switzerland, had few elements in common with Hallstatt times. Hallstatt tombs featured weapons used mostly for hunting or as decorations, but La Tène graves were filled with weapons made for war. Swifter two-wheeled chariots replaced the earlier wagons with four wheels. The one thing that remained the same was drinking gear either imported from or inspired by Greek and Etruscan artisans.

We don't know exactly what happened to end Hallstatt dominance, but we can make a pretty good guess. Sometime in the early fifth century B.C., the Celtic tribes who had been living on the northern frontier were growing restless. They had been constantly fighting the fierce Germans and receiving only what few secondhand luxury goods trickled north from Hallstatt lands. For generations the northern Celts had gained plenty of fighting experience as they held back the Germans—all the while watching their alpine cousins enjoy Greek wine and Etruscan luxury goods. The Hallstatt Celts must not have known what hit them when the northern tribes rolled in on their two-wheeled chariots. Within a generation the Hallstatt way of life was over—and the focus of the Celtic world shifted north.

It may be no coincidence that at the beginning of the La Tène era, the Greeks started to notice the Celtic world of central and northern Europe. The shift from Hallstatt to La Tène certainly would have captured the attention of Greek merchants, who probably passed their information on to the Aegean. The historian Herodotus in the mid–fifth century B.C. is the first Greek writer to mention the Celts. In explaining the course of the Nile in Egypt, he compares it with the Danube (Greek *Ister*): "For the Ister begins in the lands of the Celts and the city of Pyrene, flowing through the center of Europe." Herodotus's geography isn't as clear as we would like, but he does correctly place the source of the Danube squarely in Celtic lands, near an unknown settlement of Pyrene.

THE ART we find in La Tène tombs is stunning. It builds on the eastern and Mediterranean influences seen in Hallstatt graves but takes craftsmanship and imagination to a whole new level. The La Tène style would last for centuries and has come to define the essence of Celtic art. From its beginnings in the fifth century B.C., it flourished in Gaul until the Roman conquest and survived in Ireland even into illuminated medieval manuscripts such as the Book of Kells.

Words cannot do justice to the beauty of early La Tène torques, scabbards, and drinking vessels. All the artistic ele-

ments of the Eurasian steppes, the classical Greeks, and the in-
genious Etruscans were combined with an ancient native Celtic
tradition to form a style that was more than just the sum of its
parts. An early fourth-century drinking flagon from Basse-Yutz,
France (see photo insert), superbly captures the spirit of La
Tène art. The Greek and Etruscan influences of this coral and
red enamel inlaid beaker are clear, but the native Celtic artist
also added an eastern focus on intricate details for the highly
stylized animals on the rim and handle—which seem to be
sneaking up on a tiny duck sitting on the spout.

Countless other examples could illustrate the artistic revolution of the La Tène Celts in this early period. But the skill and
innovation of Celtic craftsmen were just one aspect of a culture
beginning to burst out of its traditional boundaries. The warriors of the Celtic tribes were starting to realize their tremendous potential as fighters at the same time as their population
was rapidly rising and in need of new lands. As they looked
southward from their traditional homeland, they cast their eyes
covetously on the rich Mediterranean world. Why be content
with imported goods and overpriced wine brought by traders
when they could go to the source and take what they wanted by
the strength of their swords? The Etruscans, Romans, and
Greeks were about to see firsthand the awesome power of these
formidable barbarians—the Celts were on the move.

THREE

DELPHI

In days to come a battle will befall us all,
when late-born Titans will rouse the Celts
with barbarian swords against the Greeks,
rushing from the distant West.
CALLIMACHUS, *HYMNS*

THE FIRST THING Posidonius would have done before beginning his journey west to the land of the Celts was to search through all of Greek history and ethnography to learn everything possible about these strange people. Any reference to the Celts in Herodotus, Xenophon, Polybius, or a dozen other authors would have been carefully sought out and recorded. It wasn't that Posidonius was ignorant of the Celts—everyone knew something about them—but it was vital that he separate fact from fiction before starting his own exploration. Contemporary Greek tales of the Celts as war-mad boogeymen may have had a basis in truth, but Posidonius knew there had to be more to the story. In any case, to be forewarned was to be forearmed. In spite of the risk, Posidonius was driven by his insatiable intellectual curiosity to see the Celts of Gaul for himself. The more he could learn about them before visiting, the better chance he had of returning home alive.

POSIDONIUS would have known the writings of Herodotus well, but the historian's brief placement of the Celtic tribes somewhere at the head of the Danube was not a great help in preparation for his journey. For more than a century after

Herodotus, there are only tantalizing hints about the Celts in Mediterranean writings. The Athenian aristocrat Xenophon mentions Celts as soldiers hired by the Sicilian king Dionysius to fight in southern Greece in 369 B.C., but he describes little more than their presence in the army. In the middle of the fourth century B.C., the Celts were known well enough to Greek audiences to be mentioned in a comic play by Ephippus, but only as inhabitants of the far west. A much more interesting source is a fragmentary Greek inscription from 352 B.C. found in the ruins of an old temple on the Athenian Acropolis. On this stone there is a long list of valuable items stored at the temple treasury, such as copper helmets and tiaras. But two short words—*sidera Keltika* (Celtic iron weapons)—appear halfway down the back side of the stone. How these armaments, presumably swords or daggers, wound up on a hill in Athens at this early date is a mystery. They may have been trade items, weapons captured in war, or gifts from a visiting embassy. But they provide marvelously direct evidence that the value of La Tène craftsmanship was being recognized far from the Celtic heartland of central Europe.

Information useful to Posidonius on the culture and personal habits of the Celts begins in earnest with none other than the philosopher Plato, writing his final work, the *Laws,* in the mid–fourth century B.C.. Plato was always dreaming of an ideal city, free from vices such as greed and drunkenness. According to the philosopher, the Celts—along with most other barbarian tribes—loved wine to an excessive degree. We don't know whether Plato is just lumping the Celts in with foreign tribes indiscriminately or actually knew something of the brisk trade in Greek wine with the Celtic homeland. In any case, the Celtic love of strong drink became proverbial for centuries thereafter. The description must have been sobering for Posidonius. The only thing worse than a journey among barbarians was one among drunken barbarians.

Plato's student Aristotle, in the late fourth century B.C.,

makes several intriguing observations about the Celts. First, he states that the Celts, unlike most warlike cultures, openly approve of sexual relations between men. Homosexuality was common in the Greek world, but the Greeks always seemed amused to find it elsewhere. Some British scholars in the nineteenth century dismissed Aristotle's comments on the sexuality of their Celtic ancestors as slander, but this negation conveniently ignores later classical authors—such as Posidonius himself—who describe homosexuality among the Gauls in some detail. But Aristotle's second claim about the Celts was a common motif found around the world in descriptions of hardy cultures—that they dip their newborn babies in freezing rivers to harden them early to the difficulties of life. Aristotle's final comments are particularly interesting: "For the sake of honor, a virtuous man will stand his ground and perform brave deeds. But someone without any fear at all—not even of earthquakes or waves, as they say of the Celts—moves beyond bravery into an undesirable quality without a proper name . . . best called madness."

Aristotle later compares the Celts to those who foolishly taunt thunderbolts in a lightning storm. He even mentions a snippet of an otherwise unknown story of Celts vainly attacking the raging sea. These sayings and stories must have been based, however distantly, on some direct information about the Celts. They would be echoed again and again in later Greek and Roman authors portraying the Celts, fairly or not, as a people who did not know when to give up. To a Greek, bravery was all well and good, but there came a time when even the mighty Achilles turned and ran. Balance was the ideal in all aspects of Greek life—eating, drinking, even fighting. A person, like the proverbial Celt, who didn't know when to call it quits was not admirable, only foolish.

Posidonius would have also read the works of the fourth-century B.C. Greek historian Ephorus, whose *Universal History* survives only in fragments. Ephorus had a particular interest in the western Mediterranean and mentions the Celts on more than one occasion. Most of his comments are brief geographical notes, but he picks up the idea of Aristotle that the Celts were unafraid of ocean waves. He reports the frankly bizarre story that the Celts would stand by their oceanside homes in fierce storms and needlessly perish along with their houses. Other Celts, he says, withdraw from the shore and then rebuild their houses on the same vulnerable spots as an exercise in patience. How these stories arose is uncertain, but they may be based on a tiny thread of truth. Later stories say that the Cimbri—a Germanic tribe living in what is now Denmark—were driven from their low-lying homeland at about this time by a series of fierce floods. By the time the story was retold repeatedly on the way south, it may have become a proverb about Celtic foolishness in the face of storms. Whatever the origin, stories of irrational Celtic behavior were favorites in the Greek world and could not have given much comfort to Posidonius.

Another comment by Ephorus is more believable and much more amusing: "The Celts . . . are very careful not to become potbellied or fat. If any young warrior develops a belly that sticks out over his belt, he is punished." This is a very practical dietary rule for any warrior culture that depends on swiftness of sword and foot. The medieval Irish Celts had a similar no-nonsense law for encouraging a slim physique among fighting men—any woman could divorce her husband without question if he became too fat to perform sexual intercourse comfortably.

One final passage from a little-known Greek playwright named Sopater must have given Posidonius great pause. About 300 B.C. Sopater had a character in one of his plays humorously vow to burn alive three scholars as an offering to the gods "in imitation of the Celts." This was written to give audiences in Greek theaters a good laugh, but there's no reason to doubt that this earliest reference to Celtic human sacrifice was anything but real—as Posidonius was soon to find out for himself.

o o o

THESE EARLY COMMENTS on the Celts were scattered and few. There was no reason for the Greek world to be particularly concerned about the Celts in the years before and even decades after Alexander the Great. To any Greek, the Celts were just another race of distant barbarians. Traders might bring back stories of them, and occasionally a small group of Celtic warriors might appear among the mercenaries of a hired army, but they were no threat to civilized Greek folk going about their daily business.

At the beginning of the third century B.C., however, everything suddenly changed. The Celts marched in mass into the very heart of the Mediterranean world.

THE CELTIC warriors who appeared at the Greeks' doorstep in 279 B.C. were part of a huge explosion of La Tène Celts eastward out of central Europe starting about 400 B.C. At this time, a great migration began down the Danube River from the Celtic homeland. Celtic grave goods had begun to show up in cemeteries in present-day Slovakia, Hungary, and Romania by the mid–fourth century B.C. The picture that emerges is not one of a Celtic swarm descending on the native inhabitants of the northern Balkans, slaughtering all who stood before them. There was a huge influx of Celtic warriors, farmers, and families into the new areas along the Danube, but the invasion seems to have been waves of immigration and settlement alongside indigenous cultures rather than a wholesale replacement of population.

By 300 B.C., the La Tène culture of the Celts stretched from the shores of the Atlantic to the forests of Transylvania. But the Celts were not satisfied to stop at those boundaries. In the early third century B.C., breakaway groups had made their way to southern Ukraine and even as far as the Don River in southern Russia. There they left their La Tène jewelry and weapons in graves along the shores of the Black and Caspian seas, far from the alpine lands of their grandparents.

Other Celtic groups moved southeast into the northern' Balkans to the lands of the Illyrians and Thracians. With these two tribes, the Celts found adversaries who shared their reputation for bravery and their love of raucous feasts. One story recorded by the Greek historian Theopompus shows us an unexpectedly devious side of the Celts in gaining an unfair advantage over the Illyrians. A group of Celts invited enemy warriors from a nearby Illyrian tribe to a grand feast, claiming it was time to put conflict behind them: "But the Celts, knowing the Illyrians loved to overindulge at banquets, slipped a medicinal herb into their food that attacked their bowels and gave them a violent case of diarrhea. Some of the Illyrians were caught and killed by the Celts, but others were overcome with pain and drowned themselves in a nearby river."

The wealth of La Tène archaeological finds from this era along the lower Danube to the north of Macedonia and Greece shows that there were a huge number of Celts living just beyond the borders of the classical world in the early third century B.C. But the heirs of Alexander's empire still strongly guarded their northern frontiers and kept away any troublesome Celts who tried to raid the rich lands of the south. The Celtic warlord Cimbaules made a try against the Macedonians as early as 298 B.C. but was soundly driven back before he could reach the Aegean Sea. But by 281, the political situation had weakened enough in Macedonia for the Celts to try again.

The story of the Celtic raid on Greece over the next two years is told by several classical authors, but our best source is the Greek writer Pausanias, who interrupts his second century A.D. travel guide to Greece to give a detailed history of this first great meeting of the Celtic and Greek worlds. According to Pausanias, veterans of Cimbaules's failed expedition regaled younger Celtic warriors with tales of the wondrous riches they had seen in the south, until whole armies of Celtic infantry and cavalry along the Danube were polishing their swords and . thirsting for gold.

So many men volunteered for this great raid that the Celts—interchangeably called Gauls by this point in Greek history—divided their army into three parts. In 281, the chieftain Cerethrius led his forces southeast into the land of Thrace, just to the north and west of Byzantium. Brennus and Acichorius marched on the Paeonians to the north of Macedonia, while Bolgius headed straight for the heartland of Alexander's old kingdom. King Ptolemy of Macedonia (one of many Hellenistic kings bearing that name) roused his army and met the Celts with great bravado. But by the end of the day, Ptolemy's head was decorating the end of a Gaulish spear. The Celts of the east had launched a major invasion of the Greek world and slain one of the most powerful rulers in the Mediterranean, leaving the way open to riches beyond their imagination. But for some inexplicable reason, the army of Bolgius retreated north. Pausanias said it was a lack of courage, and the Gaulish chieftain Brennus seems to have agreed. He was livid when, after returning from his raid on the Paeonians, he heard the news of the shameful withdrawal. For two years thereafter, Brennus staged a public and private campaign to drum up support for a second raid south. Follow me, he said, and I will lead you into a weakened land rich with silver, gold, and temple offerings waiting to be plucked like ripe fruit.

Brennus chose his proven comrade Acichorius as his lieutenant and marched south in 279 B.C. with, according to Pausanias, an army of over 150,000 infantry and cavalry. Even allowing for the legendary inflation of classical historians, the Celtic forces that marched on Macedonia and Greece were numerous enough to spawn widespread panic in the cities and countryside of the Greeks.

Imagine the sight meeting the peasants tending their olive trees on the slopes of Mount Olympus in northern Greece as the first Celts rolled south. Huge marching men, each with a gigantic spear and an enormous sword hanging from his belt. The Gauls had brightly decorated shields at their sides, gleaming helmets, flowing cloaks, and a lust for plunder in their eyes. As Pausanias says, "The spirit of the Greeks was utterly broken." The Celtic horsemen as well were a marvel to behold. The cavalry with their polished and deadly gear were organized into efficient three-man units each called a *trimarcisia* (Gaulish for "three-horsemen") made up of a rider and two aides. If a horse was slain, one of the aides immediately brought the rider a new mount. If the rider was killed or injured, one of the aides took his place. In this way, the number of cavalry was constant even at the height of a furious battle. The Greeks had not faced a threat like this in the two centuries since the Persian Wars. But unlike the Persians—who wanted only submission and taxes—the Celts were out for fortune and glory by the bloodiest means possible.

The Macedonians and Greeks in the north locked themselves behind their city walls and watched as the Celts burned and looted the surrounding countryside. Brennus and his troops marched ever southward, past the ancient Macedonian capital of Pella and down the western shore of the Aegean Sea. The southern Greek cities immediately raised a mighty army to hold back the Celtic tide and sent their forces to stop Brennus at the pass of Thermopylae—the very spot where the Spartans had made a suicidal stand to delay the Persians.

The Greek leaders dispatched a cavalry unit to ride ahead of the Celts and destroy the bridges they would need to cross on the way to Thermopylae. The horsemen worked furiously to accomplish the task, but just as they finished they realized that Brennus had foreseen their plan. The Celtic general had shrewdly picked out the best swimmers in his army and sent them downstream to cross and outflank the Greek forces, who quickly withdrew. The Greeks had expected wild savages and bloody hand-to-hand combat, but instead they were faced with a barbarian general who could think his way out of a bad situation. Brennus then forced the terrified local Greeks to build new bridges and marched his main army across.

Brennus attacked the region around the nearby city of Heracleia, but he realized he needed a decisive victory over the main Greek army both to enter southern Greece freely and to convince his hesitant men they could indeed defeat the Greek soldiers in an open battle. The Celts swiftly marched to Thermopylae and launched an all-out assault on the Greek forces stationed in the pass. The result was a ferocious, slogging, weary battle in a narrow swamp that destroyed huge numbers on both sides. But the Celts, echoing Aristotle's description, didn't know how to give up. Pierced by spears and arrows, dying Celts would pull the weapons out of their own bodies and launch them at the Greeks with their final breath.

Brennus finally realized this bloody stalemate was getting the Celts nowhere. He then conceived a brilliant if brutal plan. He dispatched a contingent of his men across the mountains to Callium. If, he reasoned, he could launch a suitably savage attack on their city, he would force the Greeks from that region stationed at Thermopylae to withdraw and thus weaken the Greek position in the pass. As Pausanias reports, the fate of the Callians was unlike anything previously known to the Greeks:

> The Celts killed every male they could find, butchering even old men and infants. Fat babies were slaughtered for food and to drink their blood. Women and young virgins, if any spirit remained in them, knew what was coming when the city was captured. They were taken and abused in every possible way by men lacking either pity or love. . . . The Celts even satisfied their brutal lust on the dying and the dead.

Allowing for a large measure of exaggeration in Pausanias's account, the destruction of Callium was certainly cruel. But the plan of Brennus had its desired effect. The Greeks of that region returned from Thermopylae and weakened the allied forces in the pass. Brennus left Acichorius behind with most of the army and himself led a force around the back of the mountain above Thermopylae to encircle the Greeks—just as the Persians had done two hundred years earlier. The Greeks had been outwitted again, and they knew it. The Athenian fleet ferried the Greek army away from Thermopylae rather than perish as the Spartans had two centuries earlier.

ALL THE RICH cities of Greece—Athens, Sparta, Thebes, Olympia—now lay before Brennus, but the one he most longed to possess was the holy city of Delphi. It's not surprising that Brennus would have heard of fabled Delphi even in the far north. For centuries Greek traders had traveled among the Celts and had surely told them stories of the wonders of Greece, especially the great shrine of the god Apollo at Delphi. The physical setting of Delphi is spectacular, perched on a steep mountain slope two thousand feet above the blue waters of the Gulf of Corinth. Far above the city looms snowcapped Mount Parnassus, sacred to the Muses. Bronze Age Greeks had lived at the site, but the oracle of Apollo dates only from the ninth century B.C. For centuries before Brennus, Delphi had been the literal center of the Greek world. The great *omphalos* or navel stone standing at Delphi marked the spot where two eagles Zeus had released from east and west met. Inside the walls of the town were temples and treasuries from all the cities of Greece. Whenever there was a victory in war or in the Olympic games, cities and private citizens would dedicate memorials and golden offerings to be stored in their own treasuries at Delphi.

The centerpiece of Delphi was the temple of Apollo. Greeks great and humble would come to this sanctuary to seek the guidance of the god's oracle. At the temple of Dodona in western Greece, priests would interpret the sound of the wind blowing through oak leaves as a message from heaven. At Delphi, the process was more dramatic. A supplicant would perform an offering outside Apollo's temple before the consultation began.

If the signs from the sacrifice were good—such as the animal acting properly while water was sprinkled on its head—the inquiry of the god could proceed. The priests escorted the visitor into the inner sanctuary, where a sacred prophetess of the god, known as the Pythia, sat hidden on a tripod. The Pythia was an ordinary woman, sworn to perpetual virginity, who served as a conduit from the god throughout her life. Shaking laurel leaves and perhaps inhaling hallucinogenic vapors from a crack in the earth, she responded from her trance to any question that was posed. Whatever inspired words she uttered were interpreted by the attending priests and put into poetic form. The final verses were often obscure and open to various interpretations. In the sixth century B.C. the Lydian king Croesus sent ambassadors to ask the Delphic god if he should attack the rising Persian Empire. The oracle responded:

If you attack the Persians,
A mighty empire will fall.

This was just the answer Croesus had hoped for. It was only later, as he stood tied to a Persian stake about to be burned alive, that he realized the oracle had meant his own empire would end if he went to war.

But Brennus was not interested in consulting the oracle. It was the rich treasuries of the Greek cities at Delphi that fired the insatiable greed of the Celts. The Celtic general joked that the immortal gods were generous and ought to share their treasures with men. Brennus was so eager to take Delphi that he didn't even wait for Acichorius and the rest of the army to catch up. Dividing his forces in this way was the first mistake Brennus made. As Acichorius trailed behind, local Greeks harassed his troops from the hills and killed many of the Celts.

The inhabitants of Delphi at this time, reinforced with a few soldiers from neighboring towns, were in an absolute panic.

Should they abandon the sacred city and its treasures or stand and fight the barbarians to the death? They consulted the oracle of Apollo, who—in unusually plain language—told them to stay put and not destroy the food and drink in surrounding farms as they had planned.

When Brennus arrived the next afternoon after a long march, he debated his next move. Some of his lieutenants urged him to attack Delphi immediately, before the townspeople could gather their courage and perhaps bring in more troops. But the Celtic warriors were tired and hungry. Pausanias reports that thunder and earthquakes held the Celts back from attack that night, but it's much more likely that Brennus wanted to give his soldiers a much-needed rest before the assault. This was his second mistake. The Celts immediately raided the nearby farmhouses full of wine and proceeded to drink themselves into a stupor.

The next morning, thousands of severely hungover Celtic warriors stormed the walls of Delphi. It was a terrifying battle of desperate Greeks fighting for their lives against ferocious Celts longing for gold and glory. In the middle of the fight, priests of Apollo ran to the front lines claiming they had seen the god himself come down from the heavens to join in. Whether the Greeks believed it or not, they redoubled their efforts to repel the invaders. At this crucial point in the attack, Brennus himself was wounded and carried off the field. It was enough to shake the confidence of the Celtic army and allow the Greeks to repel the enemy from the walls.

Disheartened, exhausted, and far from home, the Celts began their long retreat north. Along the roads and mountain trails, they faced constant guerrilla attacks from local Greeks who had suffered from the Celts on their previous march south. Brennus could no longer stand the pain of his injuries and the guilt of a failed invasion he had so forcefully advocated. He drank as much as he could of undiluted wine, then killed himself with his own dagger. Pausanias and other historians claim that not a single Celtic warrior survived the march back to the Danube. The inhabitants of Delphi were so thankful for being spared from the Celtic hordes that they inaugurated a festival to be held every four years thereafter.

But this may not be the whole story. Another tradition claims that the Celts succeeded in taking part of Delphi and carried north untold riches. This treasure eventually made its way back to Gaul, where it was ritually deposited in a lake near modern Toulouse. In 106 B.C. the Roman general Caepio reportedly appropriated the riches for personal gain and ended up in shameful but luxurious exile. Whether or not Brennus and his Celts had success in their raid on Delphi, in the end the Celts did not remain long in southern Greece. But a large group—perhaps including veterans of Delphi—did settle in modern Bulgaria. Here, along the shores of the Black Sea, they formed the Celtic kingdom of Tylis. Meanwhile, other Celts cast their eyes farther to the east, to the wealthy Greek lands of Asia Minor.

POSIDONIUS must have learned many lessons about the Celts from the accounts of the attack on Delphi. All the undesirable qualities associated with barbarians—greed, drunkenness, cruelty, foolish bravery—were there, but he also discovered admirable qualities, such as cleverness, determination, and inspired leadership. The Celts were definitely not going to be a simple study for the philosopher. But the best and most reliable descriptions of Celtic behavior available to Posidonius were those concerning the Gaulish tribes that had long lived nearby in the mountainous lands of central Asia Minor bearing their name—Galatia.

FOUR

GALATIA

Oh foolish Galatians! Who has bewitched you?
ST. PAUL, *EPISTLE TO THE GALATIANS*

If you traveled back to classical times and headed inland from the Aegean Sea east to the barren highlands of central Asia Minor, the last thing you would expect to see would be Celts. But one of the most amazing and little-known stories of ancient history is that a thriving culture of fair-skinned, Gaulish-speaking, and indomitable Celts thrived for centuries in the mountains of what is today central Turkey. How untold thousands of Gaulish men, women, and children arrived at and survived for so long in a place so utterly different from their native land is a tale Posidonius would have studied carefully before beginning his journey. We can be sure he read descriptions of these Galatians by Greek historians and heard firsthand accounts of their peculiar ways from travelers. Here was a golden opportunity for him to learn about Celtic customs, religious beliefs, social organization, and language. The records and rumors that Posidonius had at his disposal were often biased, but enough truth shines through to provide a remarkable glimpse of a vanished people.

IN THE YEAR 279 B.C., when Brennus and his warrior hordes were heading south to Delphi, two Celtic leaders, Leonorios and Lutorios, split away from their kinsmen and soon led three Celtic tribes eastward to the Bosporus strait dividing Europe from Asia. Lutorios moved south and slipped across into Asia Minor near the ancient ruins of Troy. Leonorios led a larger force, probably including women and children, to Byzantium. There he struck a deal with King Nicomedes of Bithynia—in exchange for free passage, the Celts would serve as allies and soldiers for Nicomedes. As long as the Gauls avoided Bithynian territory, they were free to ravage and raid Asia Minor to their hearts' content.

Once the Celts had taken care of Nicomedes' enemies (which took less than two years), they behaved like foxes in a henhouse. The first tribe, the Trocmi, were allotted the lands on the north coast of the Aegean; the Tolistobogii chose the rich cities of the central coast, from Pergamum to Ephesus; the third tribe, the Tectosages, raided the inland towns. Miletus, Ephesus, and many other rich cities were attacked or destroyed over the next few years. Greeks who had heard about the Celtic raid on Delphi now saw firsthand the terror of Gaulish warriors storming their walls. (Although these cities were located in modern-day Turkey, they were all Greek settlements.) Some cities bought off the Gauls, at least for a little while, with generous payments of cash, but others fought back. Greek inscriptions from the time record the heroic deeds of citizens who rose to protect their towns. One stone relates how Sotas of Priene, just north of Miletus, organized his fellow citizens to drive off the Galatians, who had reportedly destroyed the countryside, burned temples to the gods, and tortured captive prisoners.

An ancient Greek poem traditionally attributed to a woman named Anyte portrays a scene from a besieged city that, even if imaginary, must have been all too real in many towns:

O Miletus, our beloved home, now we must abandon you
and escape the barbaric lust of the godless Galatians.
Against our will, we citizens, three young virgins,
forced by the savagery of the Celts, have come to this sad end.
We would not give in to such a wicked fate, an unholy wedding,
but we choose instead a marriage with Hades.

Many Galatian fighters took women as slaves from the cities of Asia Minor. We know that some slaves were ransomed, but others never saw their families again.

The Celtic raids on Greek cities continued for years while the rulers of Asia Minor blamed one another for the resulting chaos. Finally, sometime around 270 B.C., King Antiochus I raised a huge army and defeated the Celts decisively near Sardis. The grateful Greek cities awarded him the title *Soter* (savior), the same Greek word later used by Christians for Jesus. At this encounter, the Galatian warriors saw something they knew only from childhood tales back in Europe. Antiochus used trained elephants to spread panic and to trample the Celts, as seen in a victory figurine from the time showing an elephant crushing a Galatian warrior beneath his massive feet. This celebrated Battle of the Elephants marked the end of the Celtic looting spree on the Aegean coast. The Galatians, however, were down but not out.

AFTER the Battle of the Elephants, the Galatians migrated hundreds of miles inland to the isolated highlands of central Asia Minor. This was an area once occupied by the mighty Hittite Empire and later by the Phrygians, but by the time of the Galatians it was a sparsely settled land far from most major trade routes. From their mountain strongholds, the Galatians were perfectly positioned to cause trouble throughout Asia Minor. They offered their services as mercenaries to whatever kingdom paid the most. When the Galatians weren't fighting in a foreign army, they terrified surrounding regions until bought off by a frightened king. The kingdom of Pergamum on the Aegean regularly paid tribute to the Galatians until the 230s, when the citizens grew weary of this costly protection racket. As soon as the money stopped, the Galatians descended from the hills. However, the army of Pergamum under Attalus I met and crushed the Galatians in a victory so unexpected and decisive that it was celebrated in some of the most famous sculptures of the Hellenistic age.

The originals of these bronze statues have not survived, but Roman marble copies give us a fantastically detailed portrayal of Celts from the third century B.C. The most famous sculpture—the *Dying Gaul* in Rome's Capitoline Museum—shows a Galatian with wild hair and a drooping mustache leaning on his right arm with his last ounce of strength. He is naked except for a torque around his neck—typical battle dress for many Celts, as Posidonius would later see in Gaul. His sword lies at his side, as does a large, curving war trumpet. The exhausted man's eyes are cast down, past the mortal wound in his chest toward the ground to which he will soon fall. It's a marvelous portrait of a defeated yet noble enemy.

A second statue shows Galatian warrior similar to the first, but this one supports his dead wife with one arm while he plunges his own sword into his heart. This warrior has slain his wife to save her from the bitter fate of women taken in war and is now committing suicide as a final act of defiance. As the blade sinks in, he glances over his right shoulder at the Greeks off-scene who are bearing down on him. Like Brennus before him, he prefers to die a free man by his own hand rather than face capture and enslavement. It was a theme played out again and again in Celtic struggles with the classical world.

KING ATTALUS celebrated his defeat of the Celts in monuments, but he wasn't above using their services when needed. Some years after his defeat of the Galatians, he imported a whole Gaulish tribe known as the Aegosages to help maintain his hard-won kingdom. Not just warriors but Celtic women, children, and endless streams of baggage were ferried across the Hellespont to Asia Minor from Europe. The Aegosages, however, were something of a disappointment to Attalus. On September 1, 218 B.C., a lunar eclipse reportedly provoked the mercenaries to mutiny, but it was probably more than just signs in the heavens that discouraged the Aegosages. They had been ordered to subdue rebellious areas of Attalus's kingdom and were forbidden from looting cities the king considered his own. The Aegosages had been hoping for easy riches and quickly grew fed up with the situation. What was Attalus to do with thousands of disaffected Celts in his midst? He couldn't easily kill them all or transport them back to Thrace, so he settled them near Troy and told the city of Ilium to keep an eye on them. Being typical Celtic warriors, they took more naturally to the sword than to the plow and so were soon back to their old ways, this time attacking and besieging their reluctant guardians. They were eventually driven away from Ilium, but by then everyone in northwest Asia Minor was tired of the Aegosages and their marauding ways. A Bithynian army caught them in their camp and slaughtered every man, woman, and child.

MEANWHILE, the Galatians in central Asia Minor were settling into life in the classical world. The Tolistobogii chose the westernmost lands around Gordion, where legendary King Midas of the golden touch had once ruled and Alexander the Great cut through the famous Gordian knot. The Tectosages seized the center of the region, near modern Ankara, while the Trocmi settled to the east.

The Galatians preserved many of their old Celtic ways for centuries thereafter, long past the days of Posidonius. The first-century A.D. Greek geographer Strabo describes their culture and political organization during the early years:

> The three tribes all spoke the same language and did not differ from one another in any significant way. Each tribe was divided into four sections, called tetrarchies—each of these having one tetrarch, one judge, one general (under the tetrarchs' authority), and two lesser military commanders. The twelve tetrarchs together presided over an assembly of three hundred men. These all gathered at a place called the Drunemeton. The assembly judged murder cases, but the tetrarchs and judges ruled on all other disputes.

Not only did the Galatians all speak the same language but their dialect was practically identical to that spoken by their Gaulish cousins in the west. The remarkable thing about the Galatian language was not its vocabulary—we know only a few uninspiring words, such as *droungos* (snout)—but the fact that it survived so long right in the middle of the Greco-Roman world. When St. Paul wrote his New Testament letter to the Galatians, he used Greek, but many Galatians would not have understood that language. A century after Paul, Greek merchants in neighboring towns still needed interpreters to serve Galatian customers. Two hundred years later still, St. Jerome, in his commentary on Paul's letter, describes the Galatian language as similar to that spoken by a tribe he had visited in Gaul. Even in the sixth century A.D.—a full eight hundred years after the Celts had entered Asia Minor—a Galatian monk reportedly suffering demon possession was able to speak only his native Celtic tongue.

Strabo's passage is also surprising because of its political description. We might assume the Galatians, and Celts in general, were ruled over by whatever war leader could muster enough men to bully everyone else. But instead we see a more subtle system of checks and balances, with some form of democratic assembly and the subordination of military to civilian rule. The role of judges calls to mind Caesar's description of Druids in Gaul, and we have to wonder if religious leaders played some role in this Galatian system. The assembly's gathering place, the Drunemeton, is also intriguing. The word in Gaulish means "place of the sacred oak grove" and begs comparison with the Druidic places of worship among oaks that Posidonius would see in Gaul. Unfortunately, no clear evidence for Druids among the Galatians survives.

This doesn't mean, however, that there were no Druids in Asia Minor. The problem is that evidence for Galatian religion is exceedingly sparse. Passages from classical literature and inscriptions provide a few suggestions—though many date long after the first century B.C. We know, for example, that Galatian rulers were joining Greek religious cults and even becoming priests in the temples of Anatolian and Greek gods such as Cybele and Artemis. But traditions survived—in the second century A.D., at least some Galatians were still honoring gods with very Celtic names. One group near Ankara even set up an inscription in A.D. 166 proudly proclaiming that "from ancestral times, we have worshiped according to the ancient ways."

A PARTICULARLY VIVID bit of evidence for Celtic continuity has been uncovered in the last few years by archaeologists at Gordion, in the lands of the Galatian Tolistobogii tribe. Large numbers of animal bones mixed with human remains have been unearthed here. Several bodies, including a man who was strangled so violently that his spine was broken, lay in carefully arranged patterns. Another man's nearby skull still contained bits of wood from the stake that had held it high. Several women were also found with clear signs that they had met deaths from blows and strangulation. One of these was a decapitated young woman with the jawbone of an old man placed where her skull should have been. Beneath the young woman's headless body was an older woman whose legs had been severed and placed near her—along with the young woman's missing head. What is particularly intriguing about these gruesome ritual sacrifices is the season they occurred. According to an examination of the animal bones, they were slaughtered in the autumn, about the time of the later Celtic festival known as Samain—modern Halloween.

Reports of such horrific rites among the Galatians of Asia Minor must have reached the nearby Greek world. Stories were surely whispered abroad by terrified Greek travelers who had chanced to pass through Galatia on chilly autumn nights. Posidonius would have heard the tales—no doubt dismissed by many civilized Greeks as unbelievable—but on the other side of the Celtic world, in Gaul, he would see for himself that they were true.

HOWEVER STRANGE Galatian religious practices may have been to the Greeks, it was the Galatian military might that most attracted the attention of classical writers. As the ancient historian Justin says: "At that time the numbers of Galatians grew so great that they filled Asia Minor like a swarm. In the end, none of the eastern kings would fight a war without hiring Galatian mercenaries." There was evidently a population explosion among the Galatians once they were finally settled. Young Galatian men grew up hearing their fathers' and grandfathers' tales of glory in battle. When they themselves came of age, it was natural and even expected that they would make names for themselves as soldiers. Hellenistic Greek kings were constantly fighting with one another and always short of troops, so any Galatian looking to hire on as a mercenary soldier could hardly have been in a better position. The kings of the east saw a huge pool of big, tough, and willing Celts practically in their backyard, just waiting for someone to hire them. The money was good, but these soldiers were born wanderers and longed to see the world as well.

The Galatians, like most ancient mercenaries, weren't particular about whom they worked for as long as the gold kept flowing. By the late third century B.C., Galatian soldiers were employed by kingdoms throughout the eastern Mediterranean, including Syria. But the Ptolemaic dynasty of Egypt was the primary employer of Celtic warriors for hire. It's hard to imagine Celtic warriors in Egypt, gazing in wonder at the pyramids and eating dates by the Nile, but thousands of Galatians served in Egypt for several centuries.

This Egyptian service began as early as 276 B.C., soon after the Galatians had crossed into Asia Minor. Ptolemy II, the son of Alexander the Great's old friend, hired a contingent of four thousand Galatians along with other mercenaries to help him fight his rebellious brother. These first Celts in Egypt were an audacious bunch—as soon as they landed, they went into rebellion and tried to seize control of Egypt from the pharaoh. Somehow he trapped them on an island in the Nile until they killed one another or died of starvation. Ptolemy was so proud of his victory against the Galatians that he even minted coins showing their defeat.

This initial experience with fickle Celtic mercenaries, however, didn't discourage the Ptolemaic kings from recruiting more. The Macedonian kings of Egypt were in a tough spot—they ruled over an enormously rich land filled with indigenous people who rightly saw them as just the latest in a long line of hostile occupiers out to exploit their country. The Ptolemies therefore employed foreign soldiers to maintain control over the natives. Mercenaries from every corner of the eastern Mediterranean and beyond, including Galatians, flocked to Egypt. These soldiers were given gold and land of their own. The Macedonians realized it was best to have colonies of mercenaries ready at hand, both to discourage native uprisings and to produce a new generation of soldiers.

Galatians served faithfully in Egyptian wars with Syria in the late third century B.C. Some returned home to Asia Minor when their terms were completed, but many others remained in Egypt for the rest of their lives. Their names are inscribed at a cemetery near Alexandria—*Antoeis, son of Aldorix; Bitos, son of Lostoiekos, a Galatian;* and many others. Celtic shields have been found at the Fayum Oasis south of the pyramids, and some off-duty Galatian mercenaries carved their names on a temple of the Greek god Horus at Thebes in Upper Egypt:

> Thoas, Kallistratos, Akannon, and Apollonios of the Galatians.
> We came here and caught a fox.

Galatians remained a staple of the Egyptian army for many years. Generations of Celtic-speaking families were born on the banks of the Nile and grew up to serve the Ptolemaic kings. It was only with the defeat of Cleopatra and the coming of Roman power in the first century B.C. that the Galatians disappeared from Egyptian history.

THE GALATIANS first encountered the Romans in the early second century B.C. as the legions moved east to pacify Asia Minor. The Roman consul Manlius led his troops into Galatia both to bring the Galatians into line and to rob them of all the treasures they themselves had stolen from the Greeks. A few Galatian leaders tried to negotiate with the Romans, but most were determined to drive these newcomers back to Italy empty-handed. The Trocmi and Tolistobogii tribes gathered their families behind a secure hill fort near Gordion and dared the Romans to attack. The Galatians didn't realize the relentless and well-organized enemy they were facing. The result was a tragic preview of Roman battles in Caesar's conquest of Gaul. The Romans stormed the walls with typical efficiency and sent the Galatians into a panicked flight. Thousands of Celtic men, women, and children were killed, while forty thousand were taken as slaves.

The Romans weren't interested in occupying Galatia, so they withdrew after they had stripped the country of every valuable they could find. The remaining Galatians regrouped both politically and militarily, but things were never the same again. The Romans ordered them to remain in Galatia and not cause any trouble in Asia Minor—terms the Galatians didn't always live up to. The Galatians would rise again as both allies and enemies of the Romans over the next century, but the days of large-scale plunder were over.

THE FINAL HURRAH of the Galatians against the Romans in the second century B.C. provides us (as it would have Posidonius) with the story of a remarkable Celtic woman—a Galatian aristocrat named Chiomara, wife of the Trocmi leader Ortiagon.

As the Greek historian Polybius tells the story: "The Romans captured Chiomara, the wife of Ortiagon, along with other Galatian women when the Romans led by Manlius defeated the Celts of Asia. But the Roman centurion guarding her abused his power and raped her."

Polybius—who wrote his history largely as a defense of the Romans—was clearly embarrassed by the man's actions and notes that he behaved most shamefully in his dealings with Chiomara. When Ortiagon eventually ransomed his wife, the centurion led her to a river where her tribesmen would pay for her release. After the Galatians had crossed over, Chiomara told them to draw their swords and kill the Roman. The shocked centurion, who was waiting greedily for his bags of gold, was immediately decapitated by one of the Galatian warriors. Chiomara took his head, wrapped it in a cloak, and marched home to her husband. Ortiagon was surprised and worried when he saw the Roman's head. Relations with the Romans were bad enough without such a provocation. He lectured her on the importance of keeping agreements, but she calmly replied that honor was even more important. Polybius says that he met Chiomara many years later, when she was old and living in Sardis. Even then, according to the historian, she was a woman of quick wits and unconquerable spirit.

In another story from about the same era, the Greek biographer Plutarch writes of a Galatian named Camma who was a priestess of the Greek goddess Artemis. The wife of a Galatian chief named Sinatus, she was renowned for her modesty, generosity, and concern for the common people of her tribe. But trouble was brewing for Camma from Sinorix, a fellow Galatian aristocrat: "Sinorix fell madly in love with Camma, but was not able to persuade or force her to be unfaithful to her husband. In his frustration he resorted to murdering Sinatus."

Sinorix apparently avoided a murder trial before the Galatian assembly and quickly began an intense campaign to win over Camma. She spent most of her time after the killing in the temple of Artemis but not, as Plutarch notes, weeping and bewailing her widowhood:

> Camma behaved in a very calm and collected manner, biding her time. Every day Sinorix came and tried to persuade her to marry him. He had many arguments that at first seemed reasonable—he was a better man than Sinatus, he had killed him only because of his great love for her—though Camma merely turned away. But it seemed as if Sinorix slowly was making headway in his arguments.

Camma's family urged her to marry Sinorix. What had happened was certainly regrettable, they must have said, but what's done is done. You have to move on with your life, and it might as well be with an important man who's passionately in love with you. Finally, Camma agreed. She sent word to Sinorix that she would marry him at the temple of Artemis. On the appointed day, she welcomed him at the door and led him to the altar, where they were to share a traditional drink to seal the marriage. Camma drank first, then handed the cup to Sinorix. The Galatian prince joyfully drained the mixture of milk and honey Camma had prepared. Had he been paying closer attention, he might have noticed that it was poisoned.

When Camma saw that he had finished, she shouted with joy and threw herself on the altar, crying to the goddess: "Artemis, most honored goddess, I call on you as a witness that I have stayed alive for this day of vengeance. For the sake of my dear husband, Sinatus, I have endured each day waiting and praying for justice. Now that vengeance has come, I go to join my husband. But you, Sinorix, most evil of men, tell your family to prepare not a wedding bed but a grave!" Sinorix, stunned at this turn of events, began to feel the poison creeping through his body. He jumped into his nearby chariot and tried to vomit out the poison by driving furiously along a bumpy road. But it was too late. He soon grew weak and was carried to bed, dying that evening. Camma lasted just long enough to hear of Sinorix's death, then passed away in peace.

POSIDONIUS had much to learn from the Galatians. They were fierce and adventurous, and they practiced a religion beyond the imagination of any civilized Greek. They adapted to new situations yet valued tradition. Galatian women possessed a steely intelligence and would stand up to any man. All these lessons were to serve Posidonius well in Gaul. But at last the time had come to put aside books and begin his journey. The Celtic lands lay to the west—and all roads in that direction led to Rome.

FIVE

ROME

The Celts had countless horn and trumpet players making a deafening sound, while the Celtic warriors all let out a horrendous battle cry at the top of their lungs. To the terrified Romans soldiers, it seemed as if the very hills around them were alive and screaming.

POLYBIUS, *HISTORY*

WE DON'T KNOW exactly when Posidonius began his great journey to the land of the Celts. The details of his life, especially the early years, are so sketchy that it's hard to hang a firm date on anything he did. We do know that he was educated at Athens by the Stoic philosopher Panaetius, who died in 109 B.C. We also know that he was part of an embassy from Rhodes to Rome in 87 B.C. To be of an appropriate age to study under Panaetius, Posidonius must have been born in the mid to late 130s B.C. He also needed time to study in Athens, then establish himself as a teacher and respected citizen in Rhodes before being trusted as part of an important diplomatic mission to the Romans in 87 B.C. Thus the best guess at the time of his Celtic journey would be the early 90s B.C. when Posidonius was in his thirties. It was a proper age for such an adventure—seasoned but not stodgy.

Events in the Roman west would also have affected the timing of the trip. The marauding Cimbri and Teutones tribes from the far north had caused widespread panic in southern and central Gaul from their first appearance in 110 B.C. to their final destruction by the Romans in 101 B.C. During these years, not even the most daring Greek philosopher would have set foot in Gaul. In ad-

dition, Posidonius needed until his thirties to find the financial
backing required for a major expedition. We have every reason to
think Posidonius came from a comfortable background, but a long
journey needed sponsors who would donate considerable
amounts of cash for transportation, guides, assistants, supplies,
and, of course, gifts for Celtic chieftains along the way.

We also don't know precisely where Posidonius went on his
trip. Rome and Italy are mentioned as stops in the fragments of
his journey that survive, as is Cádiz, on the west coast of Spain.
He didn't sail directly from Spain to Gaul, as he might have
hoped, but was blown off course for three long months to the
Balearic Islands and African coast before reaching Italy. Then—
presumably after a much-deserved rest—he set out by road up
the west coast of the Italian peninsula. He passed through the
rocky land of the Ligurians and made his way to the ancient
Greek colony of Massalia (modern-day Marseilles), in southern
Gaul. We know that he then ventured north of civilized southern Gaul into the wilder areas beyond the Roman frontier, but
we have to look very carefully at his fragments to make an intelligent guess at just how far north he went. After a considerable
period of time, probably several months, Posidonius made his
way back to Massalia, then home to Rhodes.

ROME was naturally the first stop for Posidonius, because most
ship traffic from Greece to the west was commercial trade to the
markets of Rome and Italy. There were no passenger ships in
the ancient world, so Posidonius—like Cicero, St. Paul, and
everyone else traveling in classical times—purchased space on a
cargo ship. Accommodations were usually simple, stoic in fact,
but functional. A small, dark room and a hard wooden bunk
were all your fare bought. If you wanted food, you brought your
own or paid extra to eat with the crew. We don't know who else
Posidonius took on his journey, but it would have been unthink-
able at the time to travel without at least one slave to perform
all the menial tasks of life.

Posidonius must have been excited to arrive in Rome for the first time. As a student of Polybius, he knew the history of the city that was fast seizing control of the entire Mediterranean. Not that Posidonius would have felt any great affection for the Romans—they were, after all, taking away the precious freedom the Greek cities had enjoyed for centuries. Rome had been marching around Greece for decades, destroying cities, stealing works of art, and co-opting Greek aristocrats to promote Roman interests in the Aegean. Posidonius would have felt toward Rome the same mixture of fascination and distaste as would an Indian prince visiting Victorian London. The Greeks looked down on the Romans as unsophisticated newcomers on the world stage, but very powerful players who had to be reckoned with. The Romans had similar mixed feelings about the Greeks. They respected and admired the philosophy and literature of Homer's heirs, but they sneered at the Greeks as untrustworthy weaklings. In Latin plays of the time, the stock character of the sneaky, manipulative slave was always cast as a Greek. However, as the Romans themselves said, they captured Greece by force, but Greek culture in turn captured them. Roman schoolboys studied under Greek tutors, read Herodotus and Plato, and learned to speak fluent Greek. Even the Greek gods were being recast with Roman names.

Posidonius had arrived at the capital of an expanding and immensely powerful but deeply troubled empire. In the years when he was growing up, populist politicians such as the Gracchi brothers were challenging the ancient Roman aristocracy in a bid to redistribute power and land. The Gracchi were murdered, but the turmoil didn't die. Part of the problem was that Rome was using small-town rules to run a burgeoning empire. It still relied on nonprofessional armies from its own citizens and allies, even though this meant years away from home for the average farmer turned soldier. In the old days, a Roman man could fight against a nearby town, then be back home by harvesttime. Now rural children grew up without fathers, wives without husbands, and debt drove many

poorer citizens out of the countryside into the teeming city of
Rome. When Posidonius was still a student in Athens, Gaius Marius was elected consul for the first of seven times and pushed
through civil and military reforms that left the tradition-loving
members of the Senate screaming for blood—and this is not a colorful metaphor. Politics in ancient Rome were frequently conducted by shameless bribery, brutal intimidation, and gangs of
off-duty gladiators hired to beat up or kill one's rivals. But fear
that the Cimbri and Teutones then ravaging Gaul would find their
way to Italy kept Marius in power, along with the disruption
caused by a massive slave rebellion in the city's breadbasket of
Sicily. Once Marius had defeated the Teutones in 102 B.C. and the
Cimbri the next year, followed by the end of the Sicilian Slave War
in 100 B.C., the Romans could fully vent their spleen on one another once again.

It was at this tumultuous setting that the philosopher from
Rhodes arrived. Romans were nearly as foreign to him as Celts,
so he surely spent a good deal of time visiting Romans of all social backgrounds and exploring the sights. Posidonius was impressed with the frugal nature of the old and modern
Romans—frugality being an admirable quality to a Stoic
philosopher. He writes in his *History:* "Even in current times,
wealthy Romans train their sons to prefer water to wine and to
eat whatever is at hand. Often a mother or father will ask a son
if he wants pears or walnuts for dinner. Then, when he has
eaten just a few, they send him off to bed." During his visit,
Posidonius also needed to learn everything he could about
Roman contacts with the Celts. After all, the Celts had been in
Italy long before they attacked the Greeks at Delphi in 279 B.C.

ONE THING Posidonius didn't know—in fact no one knew
until recently—is that a small group of Celts had been living in
Italy long before the great La Tène migrations of the fourth
century B.C. Far in the north of Italy, near Lake Como, a group
of people known to archaeologists as the Golasseca culture lived

in the shadow of the Alps. They had been there since at least 1000 B.C. farming and trading on both sides of the mountains. By the seventh century B.C. they came into contact with the Etruscan culture that was spreading beyond the Apennine spine of Italy north across the Po River valley. Later Romans called these people the Lepontii—modern scholars know them as the Lepontic people. Beginning in at least 600 B.C., Lepontic speakers were carving their language on stone markers in a script borrowed from the northern Etruscans. Archaeologists have uncovered just over one hundred Lepontic inscriptions written—to everyone's surprise—in an early dialect of the Gaulish language. One reason this was so unexpected is that 600 B.C. is amazingly early for any form of Celtic to have been written down. These stone markers are, in fact, contemporary with the earliest Latin inscriptions yet discovered.

Most Lepontic stones are simple grave markers or dedications on jars. One inscription, discovered in 1913, declares:

Deu constructed this tomb and dedicated this monument
to Belgos.

Belgos was a common Celtic name north of the Alps as well, giving rise to the famously warlike Belgae tribe (and modern Belgium). Gravestones always give readers an intimate look at the past, far removed from the sweeping narratives of historians—though such stones sometimes raise more questions than they answer. Was Belgos the father of Deu, or the brother, or even a son who died in the prime of life?

Other Lepontic inscriptions have a lighter tone, such as a short dedication found on a vase:

For Latumaros and Sapsuta—Naxian wine.

Like their Hallstatt and La Tène cousins to the north, the Lepontic people enjoyed imported Greek wine, in this case from the Greek colony of Naxos in Sicily. Not only does this tell us something about how they spent their leisure time but it shows the long-range trade routes passing through this alpine region.

The Lepontic Celts never disappeared. They eventually became the powerful Insubres tribe, who would face the Romans in battle along with other Celts. But unlike the hordes of their Gaulish relatives who were about to move into Italy, the Lepontic people could claim they had been there all along.

THE SAME La Tène migrations that swept the Celts eastward down the Danube to the Black Sea, Greece, and Galatia also flowed south over the Alps into the fertile valley of the Po River in northern Italy. In time, the whole region between the Italian Alps and the land of the Etruscans came to be known to the Romans as *Cis*alpine Gaul—that is, Gaul *this* side of the Alps. North across the mountains was the original Celtic homeland, *Trans*alpine Gaul.

It's fascinating to look at how later Romans viewed the great Celtic migration into Italy. Today we have archaeological records that help us trace the movement of Celtic tribes from Transalpine Gaul into the Po valley, but Roman historians like Livy, writing in the late first century B.C., had only old stories and active imaginations. Still, some of the tales Livy used in his account do go back to very early times and shouldn't be dismissed out of hand. But Livy, like many classical historians, had a strong moralizing bent to his writing—he tried to teach his contemporary Romans lessons from history about the proper way to live.

The first few books of Livy's history are taken up with legendary stories of Romulus and Remus, early Roman kings, the rape of Lucretia, and the like. But when he gets to the early fourth century B.C., there is a noticeable shift to a more historical point of view. Plenty of mythology and legend can still be found, but much of the work squares well with Greek historical sources and recent archaeology.

Livy presents two separate reports about why the Gauls

moved south into Italy. The first reads like a modern soap opera. Once there was a middle-aged Etruscan man named Arruns, who lived in the town of Clusium, north of Rome. His wife had a steamy affair with Lucumo, a young friend of Arruns. Lucumo was such a popular youth and so physically powerful that Arruns couldn't get any of his fellow citizens to help him seek vengeance. So the cuckolded husband loaded up his wagon, traveled north across the Alps to the land of the Gauls, and introduced them to the joys of wine. There's plenty more of this back home in Clusium, Arruns told the thirsty Celtic warriors, just give me a hand with this dishonorable lout Lucumo and I'll guide you into Italy.

The story of poor Arruns is more at home in Roman comedy than in history, but it does preserve the essential truth verified by archaeology that Mediterranean trade goods, especially wine, were popular with the Celts and may well have helped entice them south across the mountains. Livy's second story is slightly more believable. Once long ago there was a king named Ambigatus, who ruled over the Celts in Transalpine Gaul. Times were good, with plentiful harvests and a soaring population—so good in fact that Ambigatus sent two of his nephews out to search for new lands. The first nephew led a large group of emigrants to the Black Forest region of southern Germany. But the second nephew, named Bellovesus, chose the "far more pleasant road" into Italy. Along with countless men, women, and children from many Gaulish tribes, he marched to the foot of the Alps near the Greek colony of Massalia but was stopped by the seemingly impenetrable mountains rising before him. The Massaliotes had just arrived from Greece and were having trouble with the natives, so the Gauls chipped in and helped them fortify their new town against all enemies. In gratitude—and probably eager to be rid of this threatening horde—the citizens of Massalia led them to a nearby alpine pass into the Po valley. There Bellovesus and his band first defeated the Etruscans in battle and then founded the city of Mediolanum (modern Milan). But

Bellovesus was just the leader of the first wave. Soon the Gaulish Cenomani tribe crossed over and settled around Romeo and
Juliet's future hometown, fair Verona. More and more tribes migrated from Gaul, but when the Boii, Lingones, and Senones
tribes finally arrived, they found all the lands north of the Po
River already taken by other Celts. Thus they moved farther
south, deep into the territory of the Etruscans and Umbrians.
The Senones were the Gaulish tribe forced farthest south of all,
to the Adriatic coastal plains known to later Romans as the
Ager Gallicus or the Gallic Lands. Here they were pressed tight
against the heartland of the Etruscans just over the Apennine
Mountains—while Rome itself was only a hundred miles away.

THE ETRUSCANS were a sophisticated culture deeply influenced by the Greeks. They were masters of art and technology—
not to mention dentistry—who possessed a rich spiritual life
(about which we have only tantalizing hints) and a large corpus
of literature (now lost). The Etruscans, furthermore, had just
completed their colonization of the fertile Po valley when the
Gaulish wagons rolled in. Like rich real estate developers suddenly dispossessed by a host of squatters, the Etruscans were
beside themselves with rage. They fought back with force of
arms, but they simply couldn't resist the mass of Celtic tribes
pouring across the alpine passes.

There's a wonderful Etruscan tombstone from Bologna, south
of the Po, that shows a deceased Etruscan noble as he surely
wanted to be remembered—sword raised, he sits astride his horse
while a truly giant Gaul, naked except for his own sword and
shield, hesitates before him. Some Gauls certainly did retreat or
fall before Etruscan soldiers, but there's a good reason the Romans labeled the Po valley Cisalpine Gaul rather than Cisalpine
Etruria. The Etruscans of northern Italy died, made an accommo-
dation with the Gauls, or returned to the cities of the south.

But even the southern city-states of the Etruscans were not
safe. In 390 B.C., the Etruscans in Clusium found themselves

staring down from their walls at an army of Celtic warriors from the Senones tribe to the east. Fast riders were sent to the Romans down the Tiber River seeking help. The Romans wisely decided not to commit any troops, but they did send three young men to Clusium with the following admonition for the Gauls—the Etruscans of Clusium are friends and allies of the Roman people; therefore, you must leave or you will have to face us on the battlefield as well. The message was respectful in tone, stressing that the Romans would rather be friends with the Gauls than enemies. But once the official communication from the Senate had been delivered to the Senones, the hot-blooded Roman ambassadors decided to press things further. After the Gauls said they simply wanted a portion of the Etruscan territory around Clusium that was not being used by anyone on which to settle some of their landless tribesmen, the Romans shot back—By what possible right do you dare to march into the territory of our friends and demand land for settlement? The Gauls were shocked at the Romans' tone and responded curtly: "We carry the right on the point of our swords! All things belong to whoever is brave enough to take them." Negotiations broke off abruptly as all rushed back to camp for their weapons. The Roman ambassadors, in defiance of custom, themselves took up arms against the Gauls.

One of the Romans, named Quintus Fabius, rushed between the Etruscan lines and boldly slew one of the Gallic chiefs. The Gauls were rightly outraged, Livy says, at this breach of diplomacy and withdrew from the battle. Many of the Celtic warriors demanded that they march on Rome immediately. Cooler heads prevailed, however, and the Gauls sent their own embassy to the Romans, demanding justice and the surrender of the Roman ambassadors. The Senate was sympathetic to the Gaulish complaint but declared it could not punish wealthy and influential young Romans such as Quintus Fabius. They then referred the matter to the popular assembly, who chose to insult further the Gauls by honoring Fabius and his comrades with the office of

tribune for the coming year. Muttering dark curses and threats
of war, the Gauls returned home.

THE GAULISH attack on Rome is presented by Livy and other
historians as one of the formative moments in Roman history.
In it we see the best and the worst of human behavior, chiefly
the foolish pride of Rome, but ultimately it is a lesson of
Roman superiority over barbarians. As uplifting a story as it
was supposed to be to Roman schoolboys, a truth remains behind the tale that is hard to escape—the Romans came per-
ilously close to being wiped out forever. If the Gauls had
succeeded in their attack, as they almost did, the Roman Empire would never have existed and generations of students would
have been spared learning Latin grammar. Even with victory,
the Romans never really felt secure until, centuries later, they
managed to crush the Gaulish tribes on both sides of the Alps.

After returning to their people, the Gaulish ambassadors to
the Roman Senate reported on the insulting treatment they had
suffered. In no time at all, the Senones were on the road to
Rome, burning with anger at such injustice. A vast line of men
and horses made its way south over the Apennines and down
the Tiber River. Everywhere villages were in a panic, but the
Gauls declared that the target of their wrath was Rome alone.

The Gauls advanced to where the Allia River descends sharply
from the Apennine Mountains. There they met an ill-prepared
Roman army that had hastily formed to meet them. Wild songs
and horrible shouts filled the air from the Gaulish camp, Livy
says. The result was a massacre. The Roman lines dissolved as the
Gauls attacked, with the survivors fleeing not home to Rome,
where they might protect their families, but to a nearby town of
the Etruscans. The Gaulish leader, named Brennus, just like the
Celtic invader of Greece in the next century, was astonished at
how easily his men had defeated the Romans. The next move was
obvious—the Gaulish warriors quickly descended on Rome itself.

The Romans who had remained in the city were in a panic.

Many packed their bags and families for a getaway before the Gauls arrived. A few decided to trust in the gods and hold out on the towering hill of the Capitol, near the Forum. The priests and vestal virgins carefully wrapped the most sacred objects of the Roman people and sought refuge in nearby towns. Some of the old men, who had long ago served their city as consuls and generals, decided they could neither abandon Rome nor be a burden to their fellow citizens on the fortified Capitol hill. They put on their magisterial robes and retired to their homes in the city to face whatever fate would bring them.

The Gauls soon reached the walls of Rome to find the gates open. The first warriors to enter were cautious—everything was far too quiet. Brennus suspected a trap and ordered his men to scout out the city. But everywhere they went, the same eerie silence reigned, so the Gauls gathered back at the central Roman Forum. Above them, the Capitol was obviously occupied by a few Romans, but the hill was easily surrounded and sealed off. Then they noticed the open doors of the fine houses near the Forum, home to the distinguished citizens of the city. When they entered the first house, they saw what they thought was a statue sitting on an ivory chair: "The clothing and ornaments of the seated figure seemed more than human. His expression was sublime and majestic, like that of one of the gods." One of the Gauls moved forward and began to stroke the beard of the seated man, just to see if he was real. That was when the spell was broken. The Roman elder hit the impudent Gaul over the head with an ivory mace and was promptly cut down. All the remaining Roman nobles were quickly killed in their homes, which were then looted and burned.

The besieged Romans watched from the Capitol hill as their beloved city was destroyed beneath them. After a few days, the Gauls had completed the task and turned their eyes to the remaining Romans on the hill. An initial assault failed, as did a subsequent sneak attack foiled by the squawking of Juno's sacred geese, so the Gaulish army settled in to starve the Romans out. Sieges, however, were not really in the nature of Celtic warriors. The Gauls sent messengers to the Capitol, letting the Romans know they would be willing to withdraw for a reasonable payment in gold. The Romans were in no mood to argue, so they agreed to give a thousand pounds of gold to Brennus if he would take his army home. When the time came to weigh out the ransom, the Romans objected that the Gaulish scales were faulty. Brennus laughed and threw his sword on the scales to make them yet more uneven. *Vae victis!* he sneered at the sheepish Romans—Woe to the conquered!

According to Livy, an exiled Roman general named Camillus rode over the hill just in time to stop the payment, then defeated the Gauls so thoroughly that not one survived (a frequent theme in such stories). But ancient readers would have been as suspicious of such a Hollywood ending as we are. The truth is the Romans did get their town back, but the Senones and other Celtic tribes lived and prospered nearby for another century, a constant threat.

ROME soon recovered from the Gallic destruction and quickly began an all-out program of securing its power in central Italy. The campaigns against the Etruscan towns that had begun before the invasion of the Gauls were renewed. Roman dominion relentlessly spread east, south, and north. In the early third century B.C., Rome scored a series of decisive victories against the Celts. Soon all the tribal lands of the Senones were confiscated. The Gauls resisted, but year by year, city by city, the Romans moved northward into Celtic lands. In 225 B.C., the Celtic tribes of Cisalpine Gaul realized things had gone far enough and decided to destroy the Romans once and for all. The Boii, Insubres, and Taurisci tribes, strengthened with mercenaries from Gaul known as the Gaesatae (Spearmen), all marched south from the Po valley to capture Rome. But the Romans learned of their plan and headed north to stop them. At Telamon in Etruria, the Romans and Celts of Italy met in one of the most vicious and decisive battles of ancient times.

Polybius provides us with a wonderfully clear picture of this fateful encounter. It's an account Posidonius would have studied carefully for its detailed look at Gaulish warfare and customs. The second-century B.C. account by Polybius of the battle of Telamon is the earliest extensive report of a meeting between the Celts and a classical army. Pausanias wrote of the Gaulish invasion of Greece long after the deed, while Livy saw the sack of Rome through the filter of a Roman moralist, but Polybius comes as close as anyone can to describing the Celts objectively, on the basis of careful research and personal investigation of the battlefield. It's even possible that Polybius interviewed a few aged veterans of the battle. In any case, he used all available documents, including letters and memoirs, for his account.

The Celtic cavalry and infantry, loaded with wagons of stolen goods and many slaves, soon found themselves facing two Roman armies at Telamon. They were sandwiched between legions attacking from opposite sides but decided to use the precarious situation to their advantage. In such a position, the Gauls were able to protect one another from any attacks from behind. Back-to-back, the Gaulish army stood on a low hill, urging one another on and knowing there was no escape except victory. Facing two different Roman generals determined to crush them, they readied themselves for battle: "The Insubres and Boii wore pants and cloaks, but the Gaesatae mercenaries stood in front of the army and threw off their clothes—both out of brash confidence and because the ground was covered with low shrubs they were afraid would snag their clothing and weapons."

A fierce battle ensued, in which one of the Roman generals was killed almost immediately, but the Romans did not hesitate in their drive, though they were terrified by the huge host of Celtic warriors and the deafening noise made by their shouts and battle horns: "Horrifying too was the sight and movement of the naked Celts in the front of the line—all young, power-fully built men, wearing golden torques and armbands. The appearance of such warriors terrified the Romans but also made them greedy for their rich spoils."

The naked Gaesatae soon learned that bravado didn't work against the highly disciplined Romans. The mercenaries were vulnerable to the relentless rain of Roman arrows, causing some in sheer frustration to charge the Roman lines like madmen, only to be cut down by the legions. Others tried to retreat into the rest of the Celtic army and started a disordered panic among their clothed comrades. The Gauls began to fall back, at a disadvantage because their long swords were good for swinging and slashing when there was plenty of room but inferior to the shorter Roman swords for thrusting in close combat. The Celts defended every foot of the battlefield dearly with their blood, but in the end the Romans squeezed until the Gaulish army was destroyed.

Forty thousand Gaulish warriors were reportedly slain at Telamon, with another ten thousand taken captive. The Romans thought it was the end of trouble from Celtic Gaul, but they had not heard the last of the Celts. Many of the Gauls in northern Italy fiercely resisted the Romans for years. Only seven years after the battle at Telamon, Hannibal invaded Italy in the Second Punic War—and the Carthaginian general found many willing allies among the Celts of Cisalpine Gaul. Just as Hannibal was crushing the Romans at Cannae in 216 B.C., the Gaulish Boii trapped a Roman army and made the skull of their leader, Lucius Postumius, into a gilded drinking cup.

But in the end, the Romans, as always, prevailed. By the start of the second century B.C., Cisalpine Gaul was thoroughly pacified. The Celts who survived were integrated into Roman society and even granted coveted Roman citizenship in 49 B.C. One civic-minded Celt of the region apparently made it big in the lucrative Roman banking trade—hence his mouthful of a name, Argantokomaterekos (Gaulish for "money lender"). His bilingual Gaulish-Latin inscription reads:

> Akisios Argantokomaterekos donated this field for gods and men alike.

But just as Gauls became Romans, some of the Celtic heritage may have passed to Rome. Virgil, author of the *Aeneid,* grew up in Cisalpine Gaul in the first century B.C. and was educated in the Gaulish city of Mediolanum. Perhaps something of the Celtic bardic tradition found its way, however indirectly, into the work of Rome's greatest poet.

SIX

SPAIN

*To the Celtiberians, it is glorious to die in battle,
but they think it wrong to cremate a man who perishes in war.
Instead they believe a warrior is carried up to the gods
if he is eaten by a vulture on the battlefield.*

SILIUS ITALICUS, *PUNICA*

THE JOURNEY of Posidonius from Italy across the western
Mediterranean to Spain must have been a grand adventure. The
voyage of over a thousand miles probably carried him directly
south of Sardinia and the Balearic Islands through the Strait of
Gibraltar to his destination at Cádiz on the Atlantic coast. This
ancient Phoenician trading post was an ideal base for exploration, intelligence gathering, and scientific experiments. For a
man born far away, on the coast of Syria, and educated in the
eastern Mediterranean, it surely was a wonder to watch the sun
setting over the vast Atlantic. Like Columbus on the same shore
fifteen hundred years later, Posidonius believed that there was
nothing but water between him and distant Asia.

Of course, Posidonius—like any educated person in the ancient world—knew that the world was round. He could observe
the curved shadow of the earth on the moon during a lunar
eclipse and would have dismissed any notions of a flat earth as
superstition fit only for peasants. Posidonius in fact had used
his knowledge of the earth's spherical nature to calculate the
size of the world. He observed that the star Canopus was barely
visible on the horizon in Rhodes, while it was a few degrees
above the horizon in Alexandria in Egypt. He estimated the dis-

tance between the two Greek cities, then determined by the
angle of the star's height in Egypt that the distance between
Rhodes and Alexandria was one-forty-eighth of the distance
around the world. His result was impressively close to the actual circumference of about 25,000 miles.

Posidonius was particularly excited to be on the Atlantic
coast because it gave him the opportunity to observe something
known only by rumor and report in the Mediterranean—the rise
and fall of tides. On the Atlantic coast of Europe, tides average
several feet, but in most of the enclosed Mediterranean they average a barely discernible inch or two. Greeks as early as Homer
had heard of the mysterious ebb and flow of the outer ocean as
it moved onshore and out again twice each day. They had also
heard how tides in the Atlantic had regular monthly and yearly
cycles, but no one was quite sure why. Many had speculated on
the cause, and a few had even connected the tides to the moon,
but Spain was where Posidonius distinguished himself from the
purely theoretical musings of his colleagues. He stayed at a
house near the shore in Cádiz and actually *watched* the ocean.
Hour by hour for a whole month, he carefully measured the
fluctuating tide. Along with these measurements, he looked to
the sky and noted the phases and motion of the moon. At the
end of the month, he compared the two and came up with the
modern link between tides and the movement of the moon
around the earth. It wasn't that his idea was totally new, but if
anyone asked him why he thought he was right, he could pull
out his charts and show them the evidence.

We know from his fragments that Posidonius spent at least a
month during the summer in Cádiz and that he traveled up the
Guadalquivir River, north of modern Seville. Where else he might
have gone in Spain is only speculation. He mentions flooding in
the Ebro River of northeastern Spain south of Barcelona and in
one fragment discusses silver mining by women in the rivers of
Lusitania, in western Iberia. He also argues for the origin of a wa-
terway called the Minius, in the mountainous land of the

Cantabrians of northern Spain. Whether or not he actually traveled to any of these regions is debatable, but given Posidonius's dedication to seeing things for himself, it is at least possible. The mountains of interior Spain were not, however, the safest place for a Greek tourist in the early first century B.C. As Posidonius would have well known, all the rivers he described led to the land of the fearsome Celtiberians.

SPAIN lies at the far western edge of the classical world, but from earliest recorded history, travelers from the eastern Mediterranean made the long journey to Iberia to cash in on its rich mineral wealth. Scattered bits of Mycenaean pottery have been found in Spain, suggesting that Greeks traveled to this distant shore centuries before Homer. The Phoenicians of Lebanon claimed they had sailed through the Strait of Gibraltar—then known as the Pillars of Hercules—long before anyone else, but their port of Cádiz, in the land of Spanish Tartessus, wasn't established until the eighth century B.C. Tartessus became legendary in the imaginations of eastern Mediterranean people as the most distant place anyone could travel. In the Bible, when God tells Jonah to preach to the wicked city of Nineveh in Mesopotamia, the Hebrew prophet heads in the opposite direction, to Tarshish, another name for Tartessus.

The Greeks were never far behind the Phoenicians when it came to seeking out new markets. Herodotus says that, about 630 B.C., a Greek captain from Samos named Colaeus was sailing to Egypt when a fierce wind from the east drove him and his crew across the entire Mediterranean Sea to Tartessus. Turning misfortune into opportunity, the Greeks loaded up with Spanish goods and made a killing on the metals market when they returned to Samos. Word soon spread of this distant western land where gold, silver, and tin were just waiting for anyone brave enough to make the long voyage. Soon more Greek traders were sailing to Spain, followed by Greek cities that established colonies in the western Mediterranean.

But the land of Tartessus wasn't the end of the world to the native people who lived there. They saw themselves as part of a vast coastal community stretching from the British Isles far down the western coast of Africa. Our written sources for this area are meager, but a Latin poem called the *Ora Maritima,* written in the fourth century A.D., draws on much earlier Greek and Carthaginian documents in describing Spanish trade in the North Atlantic:

> The people of Tartessus
> sailed even to the end of the Oestrymnides islands.
> The Carthaginians and the natives
> around the Pillars of Hercules
> frequently sailed these waters.
> Four months is hardly long enough for the voyage,
> as Himilco the Carthaginian proved
> by sailing there and back again.

The Oestrymnides were probably islands off the western coast of Brittany. This means that traders from Tartessus in southern Spain were regularly sailing up the Atlantic coast almost to the English Channel. Himilco of Carthage, in perhaps the fifth century B.C., followed them on such a voyage and returned to record his adventure in a book that was eventually translated into Greek.

The possibility that the Tartessians were regularly sailing even to Ireland shouldn't be dismissed. The same *Ora Maritima* says that it was only a two-day voyage from northwest France to the "sacred" island—a place "rich in turf among the waves." In all likelihood, this is a reference to Ireland. And though more myth than history, the medieval Irish Book of Invasions does claim that the ancestors of the Irish came not from Britain or Gaul but from Spain.

DIRECT AND SECONDARY trade along the Atlantic coasts of Europe and Africa must have made Cádiz an exciting place to visit in the days of Posidonius. Strolling around the markets, he would have seen Spanish silver, amber from the North Sea, African apes, gold from Ireland, tin from Britain—and, as always, slaves on sale from many lands. From the middle of the first millenium B.C., Spain had been a meeting ground of many cultures. In the south and east, native tribes borrowed military technology from the Greeks and adapted the Phoenician alphabet to create their unique Iberian script. The Spanish on the Atlantic coast also felt Mediterranean influences, but they were more closely in touch with the maritime culture stretching along the ocean shores of Europe and Africa. In northeast Spain, the natives traded and traveled across the Pyrenees mountains, tying them to the markets and cultures of central Europe.

At some point before 500 B.C., a new people arrived in Spain. These settlers from the region of the Alps spoke a Celtic language and had many material features in common with their Gaulish cousins. Archaeologists and scholars don't know exactly when they arrived or whether they came in more than one wave, but by the time the Greeks begin to write about Spain, these immigrants were known as the Celtiberians. The Greek historian Diodorus Siculus, perhaps drawing on Posidonius, says that the Celtiberians were a fusion of invading Celts and native Iberians, between whom there were long and bloody wars before finally they merged as a single people. This mixture of cultures is borne out in the archaeological record. Celtic torques from Spain have distinctively Iberian decorations, brooches for fastening cloaks show a blending of styles, and Celtiberian warriors carried curved Iberian swords along with their typically La Tène shields.

The Celtiberians certainly did not occupy all of Spain. Along the Mediterranean coast, the native Iberian tribes dominated, as they did in the south and west. The Vascones—later known as the Basque—occupied the Pyrenees mountains and northern coast, as they had since time immemorial. But in the mountainous interior of central and northern Spain, the Celts were firmly in command. From strongholds such as Numantia, the Celtiberians were popular as mercenaries and served in Greek and other armies far from their mountain strongholds. One early Roman poet describes Celtiberian warriors much as Polybius did the Celts in northern Italy:

> They were a stunning sight,
> wearing pants, brightly colored cloaks,
> and enormous torques around their necks.

But Greeks and Romans writing about the Celtiberians emphasize repeatedly their reputation for hospitality as well as for ferocity. A guest in a Celtiberian household was under divine protection—any insult or injury to a visitor was met with a violent and often fatal response.

MUCH about Celtiberian culture is unknown and probably always will be. The only literary evidence we have are a few bits and pieces left by classical authors. The epigraph of this chapter tells how the Celtiberians believed that the souls of slain warriors would be carried up to the gods by battlefield vultures. This idea is not remotely close to anything known in Celtic religion elsewhere, though it is similar to beliefs found in Asia and native North America. The writer implies, however, that cremation was the more standard Celtiberian practice after a nonbattlefield death—a claim verified by archaeology—in contrast to extravagant Celtic entombments north of the Pyrenees. Other Greek and Roman writers delight in emphasizing the odd ways of the Celtiberians, such as their habit of using stale urine to brush their teeth.

But in just the last few years, archaeologists and linguists have given the world a new tool for peering into Celtiberian history and culture. The Celtiberians, like the Lepontic people of northern Italy, left behind a few inscriptions written not in

Latin or Greek but in their native language. Although some of these inscriptions have been known for over a century, scholars were not able to read them with any confidence until recently. Since the 1970s, new finds and intensive research have allowed linguists a clearer look into this elusive writing. Many problems and uncertainties remain, but scholars are beginning to piece together the surprising meanings behind some of the inscriptions.

Like Celtiberian culture in general, the Celtiberian language was very different from that spoken in the rest of the Celtic world. It has grammar and sounds that are older than those of the language in Gaul. For example, the q sound we have in *quick* or *queen* was lost by the time most other Celtic languages were written down, but Celtiberian still has it. In many ways, a Celtiberian visiting Gaul would have sounded as odd as someone from Shakespeare's day dropping into modern times. The script used by the Celtiberians is also very different from Gaulish. It was usually written in an alphabet borrowed from the Iberians and represented mostly syllables instead of individual sounds. This makes reading the script a true challenge. For example, Celtiberian *Ce* on an inscription can be pronounced as *ke* or *ge,* or sometimes just *k* or *g*—and that's one of the easier problems to solve. In spite of these challenges, scholars have managed to understand enough of the inscriptions to get a general idea about what they mean. This ability to read Celtiberian inscriptions is important because what little we know about this ancient people had previously been filtered through Greek and Roman authors. With the ability to read some Celtiberian writing, we can see what these Celts had to say for themselves about their lives and culture.

If Posidonius did make it into the Celtiberian areas of central Spain, he could have seen some of the very inscriptions that have been preserved for us today. In fact, most of the inscriptions we possess date from the first century B.C. One short inscription on a small bronze tablet is typical of the problems and possibilities in trying to read this ancient language. This text was discovered not in the mountains of Spain but—of all places—in Dallas, Texas. The tablet was probably unearthed by a treasure hunter in Spain before making its way through the illegal antiquities market to New York and finally to Texas. Whatever its history, the short text reveals a few interesting facts about the Celtiberians even as it raises many questions. The most noticeable word repeated on both sides of the text is *res*—a term that has to be Celtiberian for "king." The related word in Gaulish is *rix*, while more distant Latin has *rex*, and even more distant Sanskrit uses *raj*—all derived from the same Indo-European word. The front face of the tablet (the only side scholars can read) seems to say something like "To whom it may concern: May the local king please allow Rektugenos of the Ainolicans safe passage and hospitality." This is, quite simply, a passport. What's important culturally about the little tablet is that it shows the Celtiberians used roughly the same name for their leaders as did other Celts. It also reinforces the notion of Celtiberian hospitality found in the classical authors, at least for those with the proper documents.

An even more revealing inscription was discovered deep in the mountains of Celtiberian Spain and now resides in the Archaeological Museum at Barcelona. It was carved on rock in Latin rather than Iberian script—a fact that makes it much easier to read, though the interpretation of many points is still debatable. It is a dedication by the local Celtiberian people to several gods and is written in two short sections. It can be tentatively read (including a few words of unknown meaning) as:

For Eniorosis and Tiato of Tiginos, we give trecaias.
To Lugus we dedicate arainom.

For Eniorosis and Equaesos, the ogris builds an olga.
To Lugus he builds a tiasos covering.

Granted, we don't know what a *trecaias* is or who the *ogris* might be, but the rock carving at least says something very important about this group of Spanish Celts—one of the gods they worshiped was Lugus. This is important because Lugus is the one god who shows up practically everywhere else in the ancient Celtic world. The Gauls worshiped him under the same name, and, according to Caesar (who equated him with the Roman god Mercury), they honored him above all other divinities. He appears in Welsh mythology as Lleu and, most important, in Irish stories as Lug (the Shining One), the divine craftsman possessed of all skills. The Irish danced at the midsummer festival of Lughnasadh in his honor and—just perhaps—so did the Celtiberians.

A number of other Celtiberian inscriptions are known, and more are being found every few years. Many are fairly mundane texts, honoring a dead relative or marking out property lines, but each new inscription gives us a better understanding of what life was like for the Celts of Spain.

AT THE TIME Posidonius was visiting Spain, Celtiberian culture and language were still very much alive, but the political independence the Celtiberians had enjoyed for centuries had been crushed by a long series of wars against the Romans. The Romans became interested in Spain during the Second Punic War against Carthage, in the third century B.C. The Carthaginians—Hannibal's family in particular—had developed contacts with Spain that gave them an important power base in Iberia for their conflict with Rome. Once Hannibal was defeated, the Romans decided that firm control over Spain was a priority for both military security and potential profit from the country's rich natural resources. In 197 B.C., Rome annexed the eastern and southern coastal areas of the peninsula, sending only a small army to occupy what they assumed was a docile country. Many Iberians had at first welcomed the Romans as liberators from the Carthaginian yoke, but oppressive Roman practices soon turned such support to active resistance. Although the Celtiberians lay outside the new Roman provinces in Spain, they were eager to serve as mercenaries against the Romans for any Iberian tribes who called on them.

The Romans had assumed resistance in Spain would be speedily crushed by the same military that had conquered the Etruscans, Cisalpine Celts, and Carthaginians—but Spain was different. The Iberian Peninsula is mountainous and at the time had many forests perfect for concealing hordes of guerrilla troops. Spain was also much bigger than anything the Romans had tackled before, so supplying troops often meant weeks of travel from the nearest port. For much of the early second century B.C., the Celtiberians fought the Romans in both northern and southern Spain, until they were finally checked by the legions in 179 B.C. Celtiberia, however, remained a free territory. In 153 B.C., after a number of greedy and reckless Roman governors had squandered any goodwill the Celtiberians might have felt for the Romans, a new generation of Spanish Celts rose against Rome.

The Roman consul Fulvius Nobilior decided to take his troops to the city of Numantia in the heart of Celtiberia and crush these troublesome barbarians once and for all. Unfortunately for the Roman commander, the elephants he took along to terrify the Celtiberians panicked in the mountainous heights and cost the Romans any chance of victory. The next consul decided to negotiate with the Celtiberians instead of fight, buying the Romans time to pacify other regions of Spain before turning to the Celts once more. The Lusitanians of the Atlantic coast fought the Romans back for several years under the leadership of Viriathus—a former shepherd—inspiring the Celtiberians to rise once again in 143 B.C. The Romans soon murdered Viriathus, then turned their attention to the Celtiberian fortress of Numantia.

Few towns in the ancient world had the natural defenses of

Numantia—a soaring hill with a precipitously deep valley on either side. Even Alexander the Great might have given up after examining the layout of the fortress, but the first Roman commander on the scene decided it was child's play for his naturally superior troops. Instead, he found himself besieged in his own camp, forced to come to terms with the Celtiberians. The Senate revoked his treaty and sent another general—who soon found himself caught in exactly the same trap with the same result. For nine years the war against Numantia dragged on as Roman commanders full of bluster retreated with their tails between their legs, until at last the Senate sent Scipio Aemilianus. Using sixty thousand Roman troops to blockade a town holding no more than eight thousand Celtiberian warriors, Scipio squeezed and starved Numantia until it could stand no longer. When the Roman soldiers finally marched through the gates of the defeated citadel in 133 B.C., they sold all the survivors into slavery and utterly destroyed the town.

SEVERAL DECADES LATER, Posidonius visited a country that was largely defeated but not yet tamed. Wars dragged on in northern Spain until 19 B.C., but in the end Roman power was extended across the peninsula. Spain ultimately became one of the most thoroughly Romanized provinces in the empire—home to famous Latin authors and several future emperors, as well as a major source of troops for the legions. Celtiberian language and culture survived Posidonius, but by the early Christian era, the unique Celtic culture of Spain was only a memory.

SEVEN

MASSALIA

In the time of the Roman king Tarquin, some young Greek men from Pho-caea in Asia Minor sailed to the Tiber River and established an alliance with the Romans. Then they voyaged to the most distant harbors of Gaul. There—in the middle of Ligurians and wild Celtic tribes —they founded the city of Massalia.

JUSTIN, *EPITOME*

POSIDONIUS spent at least one summer in Spain, conducting research on tides and learning all he could about the native people of the peninsula, including the Celtiberians. The Spanish coast must have been as alluring to him as it is to modern tourists, but Posidonius knew the sailing season in the Mediterranean was limited. If he was going to return to Italy that year, he had to begin soon. If he waited too late in the autumn, finding a ship's captain foolish enough to risk the stormy waves of winter would be impossible and he would be stranded in Iberia until the next summer.

As knowledgeable as Posidonius was about the Mediterranean sailing season, his eagerness to stay in Spain must have delayed him longer than was wise. The next fragment we have of his journey records his ship from Cádiz to Italy being blown about by a fierce wind from the east, bouncing him around the western Mediterranean from the Balearic Islands to the north African coast. To most travelers, this storm would have been a cause for heartfelt prayers and extravagant promises to the gods, but Posidonius was instead fascinated by the shifting pattern of the winds. We can imagine the sailors desperately trying to keep

the ship from crashing on rocky shores while the Stoic philosopher calmly stood by, balancing himself on a rolling deck,
whipped by salt spray, but methodically recording his meteoro-
logical observations.

The storm finally blew the ship to the North African coast,
somewhere near modern Algeria. There the Spanish crew
mended the sails and restocked provisions before setting sail
again eastward. They must have decided to avoid any long
crossings of open water, instead opting for a coastal cruise followed by a short jump across the strait separating Carthage
from Sicily. Somewhere along the coast of Africa, they came
upon a sight that Posidonius felt compelled to record in his
notes. As he relates, the ship sailed past a small, tree-covered
peninsula. In the trees and on the nearby beach was a sight unlike any Posidonius would have seen in Syria or Greece—apes of
all ages and sizes were swinging, jumping, and howling as the
ship sailed by. Posidonius, with his customary scientific precision, noted the behavior and physical condition of the primates,
but he also did something proper Stoic philosophers weren't
supposed to do—he laughed with joy at the strange sight, just
like a little child at the zoo. It's only a small note in his fragments, but it gives a wonderfully human picture of the man.

WHEN THE FRAGMENTS of the journey pick up again, Posidonius had finally returned to Italy and made his way north
along the coast to the land of the Ligurians, near modern-day
Genoa. For centuries, Etruscans, Gauls, and Romans had
largely ignored this rocky, inaccessible corner of Italy. The Ligurians were viewed from earliest times as primitive, backward
hill people famous for robbing travelers. In the distant past,
the Ligurians had spread far beyond northwest Italy, but by
Posidonius's day they were only a defeated remnant of a once-
powerful people. We know little about them except that they
spoke an Indo-European language related to Celtic. But aside
from a few words recorded by Roman academics, such as *leberis*

(Ligurian for "rabbit"), their language and culture have disappeared.

The Romans had little patience with the Ligurians. Once they had defeated the Carthaginians and established settlements in Spain, the Roman army needed a reliable land road from Italy along the coast to southern Gaul and on to Spain. This route lay directly though Ligurian lands, so, in the early second century B.C., the Romans began a pacification campaign against the Ligurians. Over two decades the Ligurians, like the Celtiberians, fought back with guerrilla tactics from their mountain valleys. But tribe by tribe, through raids, deportation, and starvation, the Romans systematically destroyed Ligurian resistance.

Posidonius traveled north into Liguria only a few years after decent roads had been constructed in the region. The remaining Ligurian villagers were a pathetic sight to the Greek philosopher. He has little to say about the country in the surviving fragments, aside from the fact that the Ligurians didn't so much plow their stony fields as quarry them. Somewhere on the road in Liguria, Posidonius met a resident named Charmoleon, who was originally from Massalia. This Greek was a gregarious fellow who apparently took the young philosopher under his wing. Charmoleon invited Posidonius to stay at his home while he was in Liguria—surely a relief to a philosopher on a budget.

Charmoleon was eager to aid Posidonius in collecting stories about indigenous people. He told his visitor one surviving anecdote which illustrates that the Ligurians were as tough as their rocky soil. Once he hired a group of Ligurian men and women to work in one of his fields. As the day wore on, one of the women who was pregnant went into labor. Without Charmoleon noticing, she went away by herself, gave birth, and returned with the newborn infant strapped tightly to her chest. She continued to dig and move heavy rocks until Charmoleon asked why she was lagging behind. When he saw the baby, he was astounded and dismissed the woman with a full day's pay.

However impressed Posidonius was with Ligurian tenacity, the devastation still lingering from the Roman conquest must have had a powerful effect on him. Here was an unmistakable example of Roman determination and power. Just as the Romans had beaten the Celtiberians, they had ground down the Ligurians until they could fight no longer. It was an example of what would happen to Rhodes if the island ever resisted and what was surely in store for the untamed Celts of Gaul if they chose to fight against Rome.

POSIDONIUS must have traveled west from Liguria along the newly built Roman road to Gaul. He would have seen the Alps rising from the sea along the narrow and forbidding coast. From there, the mountains fell away to the north and the country turned to rolling hills before the road entered the wide plains of the Rhone River. In the easternmost part of the delta, far from the vast swamps but close enough for easy river access, lay the ancient Greek colony of Massalia. Charmoleon probably sent Posidonius from Liguria with letters of introduction to friends back in his hometown. As he entered the gates of the city, Posidonius knew he was in one of the most diverse cities of the ancient world.

Massalia was perfectly situated both geographically and culturally to serve as a meeting place for the peoples of the western Mediterranean. The town itself was set on a small peninsula surrounded by hills above a protected harbor. Just to the west was the mouth of the great Rhone River—a natural highway running from the Mediterranean Sea deep into the Celtic lands of Gaul. To the south were Italy and Sicily, with further access to the vast commercial resources of the eastern Mediterranean and Black Sea. To the west were Spain and the trade routes along the Atlantic coasts of Europe and Africa. Posidonius's contemporary the Roman scholar Varro says that Massalia was a trilingual town, with Greek, Latin, and Gaulish heard on every corner.

Massalia prospered not only geographically but politically as well. By the time Posidonius visited the Greek colony, it was surrounded by the vast Roman territory known simply as the Provincia (modern Provence). This area included all the Mediterranean coast of Gaul inland up to a hundred miles. The nearby Celtic tribes of the Tectosages, Vocontii, and Allobroges had already lost their freedom to Roman domination, but Massalia retained its independence. From as early as the Second Punic War against Hannibal, the wily Massaliots had sided with Rome. This long-standing alliance had served Massalia well. The city enjoyed Roman military protection for its booming trade, while the Romans secured a friendly and civilized base in an often hostile land.

POSIDONIUS arrived in Massalia almost five hundred years after it had been founded by settlers from the Greek city of Phocaea. The account of Massalia's early years survives only in legendary material collected centuries later, but the stories would have been well known to Posidonius. Though the tales are more folklore than history, they preserve important elements of early Celtic culture.

The story of Massalia's foundation is preserved in a fragment reportedly written by Aristotle himself, though the fourth-century B.C. philosopher was certainly drawing on earlier historians. Other authors give variants of the tale, but Aristotle's has a uniquely ancient ring to it. He says that long ago merchants from the Greek city of Phocaea in Asia Minor arrived in southern Gaul and were warmly welcomed by Nannus, the local Celtic king. Nannus ruled over a tribe known as the Segobrigi, whose name in Gaulish means "those who live in the strong hill fort"—an appropriate term for inhabitants of the citadel of Massalia. As was true of the Celtiberians and other Celtic groups, hospitality was central to the Segobrigi. Nannus invited the Greek leader—fittingly named Euxenos, "the good guest" in Greek—to stay for the wedding feast of his daughter.

Marriage throughout the ancient world was normally a matter of fathers selecting appropriate spouses for their children,
but among the Celts of Massalia, the young woman was allowed
to make her own decision. As Aristotle relates, the guests and
suitors of the girl gathered after the feast to await the arrival of
the bride to be. Finally, the young woman entered the hall carrying a bowl of water. All the suitors who had come from the
local Celtic tribes must have flashed their best smiles and
puffed out their chests, eager to be chosen by the daughter of
such a powerful king. Petta—for that was the girl's name—
walked slowly among them, carefully holding the bowl. But
then the unexpected happened. Petta walked past all the young
men from Gaul and handed the bowl of water to Euxenos. Then
Nannus stood up and addressed the crowd: Beyond doubt, he
said, it is the will of the gods that my daughter has chosen a
stranger from across the sea to be her husband. Let us not contend with the gods but accept their choice. Nannus then gave
Euxenos the land on which Massalia stood as a wedding gift.

Aristotle's story has a fairy-tale element to it, and indeed it
parallels bridal tales from elsewhere in Greece, India, and
around the world. But there may be something of both history
and Celtic myth to the foundation story. Any clever Gaulish
king of the Hallstatt era would have realized the lucrative possibilities of having a Greek trading post on his tribal lands. The
Greeks from Phocaea, for their part, would have welcomed
strong local connections both for protection and to grease the
wheels of commerce with other Gaulish tribes. Thus, even if
there was no Nannus, Euxenos, or Petta in reality, there must
have been both Gauls and Greeks very much like them during
the early years of Massalia.

But Petta's name also suggests that there is an element of
Celtic mythology woven into the story. In Celtic stories from
Ireland, women are often seen as bringers of sovereignty and divine approval to earthly rulers. Kings are forever marrying or
otherwise mating with women who somehow embody the land

itself and who offer it as a gift to the worthy ruler. The name Petta means "portion" or "share" in Gaulish and may signify that the Celtic princess is giving the stranger from the east divine sovereignty over a portion of her tribal lands in a symbolic and most powerful way. In passing down this story of Massalia's foundation, Aristotle may have inadvertently recorded one of our earliest surviving Celtic myths.

But not all of Massalia's relations with neighboring Gaulish tribes were so positive. As the years went by and Massalia grew in power, many Celtic leaders came to resent the foreign presence on their coast. Yes, commerce was important and the imported wine was especially welcome, but so was independence. After two hundred years of trade with the Greeks, many Celts may have felt they could manage business with the larger Mediterranean world without giving a generous cut to the Massaliot middlemen. So about the year 400 B.C., the Gauls decided it was time to unite and wipe Massalia off the map.

According to a story recorded by the Latin writer Pompeius Trogus in the first century B.C., the Gauls chose a minor king named Catumandus as war leader. This story again has a ring of myth to it, but we should give it some credence because Pompeius Trogus was himself a Gaul from the region of Massalia. The tale says that Catumandus (Gaulish for "war pony") surrounded Massalia with his army and laid siege to the city with great determination. But one night during the siege, Catumandus had a dream.

In a short but terrifying vision, the king saw a woman standing before him. With a most stern and fiery expression, she proclaimed that she was a goddess. Catumandus awoke suddenly and knew that he had seen the divine protector of the Massaliot Greeks. He sent messengers to Massalia suing for peace and asking permission to worship their gods inside their city. The Greeks knew all too well the dangers of allowing wooden horses or enemy generals inside their city walls, but something about Catumandus convinced them he was sincere. Through the gates and up to the highest hill of the town marched the Gaulish leader. When he entered the temple of the goddess Athena (Minerva to the Romans), Catumandus froze. There before him was her cult statue—the very woman who had appeared in his dream.

It could be that this story was just a clever bit of Greek propaganda—look, even the barbarian Gauls honor the gods of our divinely protected city—but dreams were frequent and very real links between gods and humans in Celtic religion. Athena or Minerva or whatever Celtic names she bore as a goddess of crafts and healing was as important a figure in the Celtic pantheon as she was among the Greeks and Romans. In some Gaulish inscriptions she is called Sulevia, but Caesar calls her Minerva and names her as one of the chief Celtic divinities—a kind of female counterpart to the Celtic god Lugus. She was Sulis, the goddess of healing, at the ancient thermal springs at Bath in Britain. In Ireland, she was the goddess Brigid, who lent many of her supernatural qualities to the Christian St. Brigid in later stories. Even in the seventh century A.D., St. Eligius was still warning his medieval French parishioners not to invoke Minerva when they were weaving and dyeing cloth. If Catumandus had a dream of a female goddess like his own Sulevia or Minerva standing between him and Massalia, he would have taken the vision very seriously.

MASSALIA survived the Gaulish siege at the beginning of the fourth century B.C. and continued to thrive as the major Greek outpost in the western Mediterranean. Goods from southern Europe, Asia, and Africa flowed through its docks to the La Tène Celts of Gaul and beyond. Italian wine was shipped from Massalia up the Rhone, Loire, and Garonne rivers, and all the way to the mysterious island of Britain. Celtic merchants of the time even invented the wooden barrel, a means of transporting liquid goods superior to the easily breakable ceramic jugs used by the Greeks and Romans. Tin, copper, gold, slaves, and amber in turn all poured south into the warehouses of Massalia for shipment to Italy, Greece, and the eastern Mediterranean. Massalia was indeed the hub of a huge trade network, stretching from Ireland to Egypt. But the Greeks of Massalia wanted more. All the Celtic goods passing through their port were brought south by Gaulish middlemen. The ultimate source of these products in the northern islands and coasts of Europe was out of their reach and known only through secondhand reports. If they could just find a way to sail directly to Britain, Ireland, and the Baltic Sea, the Massaliots could bypass the middlemen and stage an unprecedented commercial coup.

But there were only two possible ways for Massaliot merchants to reach the lands of northern Europe. The first was via the extensive river systems of Gaul. The Rhone led to the Loire and the Seine, then down to the coasts of the Atlantic and the English Channel. The Garonne River route to the Bay of Biscay was shorter, but all the river highways were controlled by fierce Gaulish tribes who were not about to relinquish their lucrative position as cross-shippers of northern goods to the Mediterranean. The other avenue open to Massalia was through the Strait of Gibraltar, past Tartessus, and around the Iberian Peninsula to the Atlantic coast of western and northern Europe. Aside from the prohibitive distances involved, the strait was closely guarded by the Carthaginians, who had no intention of allowing Greeks access to the Atlantic. The Carthaginians were constantly fighting with the Greek cities of the western Mediterranean and were adamant about controlling commercial traffic past the Pillars of Hercules.

But there were breaks in Carthaginian-Greek hostilities that may have allowed a resourceful Greek from Massalia to sail quietly into the Atlantic. In the latter half of the fourth century B.C., a brief period of calm between Carthage and the Greeks opened just such a window. A voyage from Massalia into the Atlantic and north to the seas around Britain would have required a man of great courage and ability. Fortunately for Massalia, one of its native sons was both ready and eager at this time to explore the unknown lands of northern Europe, a place where no one from the Greek world had ever ventured. Along with Posidonius, this man—Pytheas of Massalia—is one of the least-known explorers of the ancient world. But thanks to *On the Ocean,* Pytheas's record of his journey, published about 320 B.C., we know something about the history, lands, and people of northern Europe and the British Isles at this early time. We can be sure Posidonius knew the work of Pytheas very well. He clearly borrows from it in his own book and in any case would never have let such a valuable resource on the ancient Celts go unread. The text of *On the Ocean,* like the works of Posidonius, was lost forever in Roman times, but quotations from classical authors who read the book in its entirety have survived. Through these we can reconstruct at least some of the remarkable journey of a man who was an important predecessor and tremendous influence on Posidonius.

BORN IN MASSALIA sometime in the mid–fourth century B.C., Pytheas was a Greek raised in a very foreign land. But unlike Posidonius, who abandoned his native Syria never to return, Pytheas seems to have stayed in Massalia his whole life—aside from his great adventure to the northern seas. In the fragments of his writings that survive, Pytheas displays a detailed knowledge of mathematics, astronomy, and geography. It's almost certain he came from one of the wealthy families of the Greek colony and quite probably was part of the merchant elite of Massalia. But more than all his formal education and scientific ability, what set Pytheas apart from the other Massaliot Greeks was his insatiable curiosity. Few men would have desired to leave the security of their native cities and risk their lives on distant seas—and no one else dared to go as far as Pytheas. Greek poets may have sung imaginatively of sailing beyond the farthest sunset to the edge of the world, but Pytheas really did it.

Like any good Greek of Massalia, Pytheas would have spoken Gaulish fluently and been quite familiar with Celtic customs. And like any good son of a merchant city, he knew his way around a ship. Likely his voyage was financed by a consortium of Massaliot traders who were glad to invest in just the chance of better access to the raw materials of northern Europe. In their eyes, even if Pytheas didn't open a direct route to the rich resources of the northern lands, he would certainly gain valuable information—if he survived. So one early spring day sometime around 330 B.C., Pytheas of Massalia set sail west along the Gaulish coast. There were plenty of friendly ports for the first few hundred miles, Greek towns such as Agde and Emporium that had close relations to Massalia. But when Pytheas turned his small ship south along the Iberian Peninsula, he was entering the realm of the rival Carthaginians. The Greek explorer would have done everything possible to make himself inconspicuous as his ship slipped quietly at night through the Strait of Gibraltar. The Greeks and Carthaginians may have been at peace for the moment, but the Carthaginians would not have been pleased to see a Massaliot ship in their waters. When the sun rose on Pytheas the next morning, the endless Atlantic Ocean stretched before him.

Carthaginian influence extended well up the Atlantic coast of Spain, so Pytheas and his crew probably stayed away from land as they sailed past Cádiz and Tartessus. But eventually the little craft had to land on the western Iberian coast for water and supplies. However, spending too much time in a region still frequented by Carthaginians was risky. So as quickly as possible, Pytheas sailed around Iberia and east into the Bay of Biscay, then up the western coast of Gaul to the mouth of the Loire River.

Landing near the Loire, Pytheas would have met Gaulish-speaking villagers from the Pictones and Namnetes tribes who gave him advice about the lands ahead. These Celts had long

been trading with northwest Gaul, Britain, and Ireland, so
Pytheas eagerly learned everything he could from them. As the
explorer then headed north and west, the coast of Gaul gradually fell behind, until only a few islands were left to mark the
edge of continental Europe. The Greek geographer Strabo—always hostile to Pytheas, though he borrows from him freely—reports that Pytheas called the last of the Gaulish islands
Uxisame, a name he heard from the natives meaning "most distant place." But Pytheas wasn't about to turn back yet.

Pytheas next crossed the stormy English Channel and came
to Cornwall in western Britain. There he found tin mines
buzzing with activity—and Gaulish merchants waiting to transport the metal to the continent. Posidonius reported on this
trade in a passage certainly derived from Pytheas: "Tin is not
found on the surface, as historians say, but is dug out of the
ground. It lies in the country of the barbarians beyond Iberian
Lusitania and in the Tin Islands. It is brought from Britain to
Massalia."

The Gauls were none too happy to see a Greek threatening
their lucrative trade monopoly by sailing directly to the Tin Islands (another name for the British Isles), but the British natives were friendly enough. The language they spoke was closely
related to Gaulish, so Pytheas would have had little trouble
communicating. The Massaliot explorer must have spent several
weeks or months sailing up the west coast of the island, carefully measuring distances and tides. It would have been easy for
Pytheas to stop off in eastern Ireland as he sailed past the future sites of Dublin and Belfast, but he left no record of such a
visit. Rumors of cannibalism among the Irish may have discouraged even the skeptical and daring Pytheas from landing on the
island.

Pytheas continued ever northward through the Hebrides Islands off the northwest Scottish coast, then on to the Orkneys
("Pig Islands" in Celtic) off northeast Britain. Finally, just be-

yond the Orkneys lay the Shetlands—desolate islands pounded relentlessly by the Atlantic. Here the man from the sunny Mediterranean must have felt he was truly at the end of the world. To the north was nothing but an endless, rolling ocean. But local fishermen told Pytheas that there was in fact a land beyond their own islands. Six days distant lay the island of Thule, a place so far north that the midsummer sun never sets.

To Pytheas, consummate scientist and explorer that he was, the chance to see this distant land near the Arctic Circle was too tempting to pass up. His crew may have stayed behind in the Shetlands, but Pytheas joined the local sailors in one of the grandest adventures in ancient exploration—a voyage to Iceland. It's incredible to imagine a Mediterranean Greek from the age of Alexander the Great sailing to a land that was not rediscovered until the Viking voyages of the Middle Ages. But Pytheas's description of Thule fits Iceland better than it does any other place—an island of endless summer sunlight six days from the Shetlands, touched by drift ice even in the warmest months. There, Pytheas says, the sun vanishes for weeks in the depths of winter. How these sailors had found Iceland in the first place is a mystery, but the paths of migrating birds or a storm-blown ship could have led them to the rich fishing grounds just a week from their home.

Returning to the Shetlands, Pytheas probably sailed down the North Sea coast of Britain to the amber-producing lands around modern Denmark, but the surviving fragments for this part of the journey are too sparse for us to be certain. In any case, one day several years after setting out from southern Gaul, Pytheas and his crew sailed back into the harbor of Massalia. Pytheas had completed one of the longest voyages of ancient history and visited lands that would not be seen again by southern Europeans for over a thousand years. He quietly published the account of his travels, *On the Ocean,* but was met with scorn and skepticism by most Greek and Roman geographers for centuries. However, the scientific precision and detail Posidonius found in Pytheas were enough to convince the Greek philosopher that here was a man who had seen the northern world with his own eyes. To Posidonius, about to embark on a voyage to unknown lands himself, Pytheas was not only a valuable source of information but a model for his own travels deep into the land of the Celts.

EIGHT

TRIBES AND KINGS

Luvernius—the father of King Bituis, who was deposed by the Romans—
tried to gain the support of the people by riding throughout the countryside in
a chariot, throwing gold and silver to all the Celts who followed after him.

POSIDONIUS, *HISTORY*

JUST AS ST. LOUIS was the entry to the American West for
the Lewis and Clark expedition, Massalia was the gateway to
Gaul for Posidonius. Fortunately, the journals of Lewis and
Clark survive intact so that historians can retrace their path
through the plains and mountains to the Pacific Ocean with
some certainty. The fragmentary nature of Posidonius's writings, by contrast, makes reconstructing the route of his journey
in Gaul extremely difficult. The bits and pieces that survive
from the *History* describe people, customs, religion, and even
mythology, but very few actual places.

Nonetheless, if we learn anything from the fragments of Posidonius, it's that he firmly believed in the Greek idea of
autopsy—literally, seeing something for oneself. We most often
use the term in a medical sense, but in ancient Greece it was a
style of investigation shared by historians such as Polybius,
Pytheas, and Posidonius. Some ancient writers openly scoffed at
the need to examine evidence firsthand. They were content to
sit in a library and sort through the available sources, deciding
what best suited their purposes. But in his writings, Posidonius
constantly repeats the statement *I saw with my own eyes.*

What did Posidonius see, and where did he go? Looking
north from Massalia, the explorer had a vast area of Gaul open

to him. The Roman-controlled Province, conquered in the second century B.C., stretched along the Mediterranean coast from Spain to Italy and inland for a hundred miles or more. Up the Rhone River, Roman territory extended almost two hundred miles into Gaul, all the way to the borders of the Helvetii tribe in modern Switzerland. In the southwest corner of Gaul, the Romans already ruled over the Tectosages—relatives of the Galatian Tectosages in Asia Minor—and other Celtic tribes in the region of eastern Aquitania near the Pyrenees mountains and Spain.

Posidonius could have learned a great deal about Celtic culture from simply talking with the conquered Gauls of the Province and collecting Celtic stories in Massalia, but the evidence of his fragments argues strongly against him choosing this easy path. Posidonius describes a world of the Celts full of war, head-hunting, and human sacrifice—activities the Romans would never have allowed in their territory. And Posidonius doesn't tell just of gruesome activities of the past handed down in old stories. He describes current customs that were so primitive they made him physically sick—until, as he says, he finally got used to them. Posidonius's ethnography of the ancient Gauls is not the work of an armchair historian sitting in a Massaliot villa sipping wine. He did not travel all the way to Gaul to do what he could have more comfortably done in Rome, Alexandria, or even at home in Rhodes. No, Posidonius must have packed his bags in Massalia and headed north to see the world of the untamed Celts for himself.

BEYOND the Roman Province along the Mediterranean shore of Gaul lay a multitude of Celtic tribes stretching all the way to the English Channel. This was the land known to the Romans as Gallia Comata, or "Long-Haired Gaul," after the dominant hairstyle of the Celtic warrior classes. To the immediate north of Roman territory were the large and powerful Arverni, Bituriges, and Aedui tribes. These groups had long been in contact with the Greeks and Romans, with merchants from the Mediterranean a common sight in Gaulish towns such as Gergovia, Bibracte, and Alesia. These large and fortified settlements supported permanent colonies of Greek and Roman businessmen who lived among the Gauls as welcome guests. The tribes closest to Roman lands had even begun to build planned cities and establish extensive, complex states based on a model more Mediterranean than Celtic. Gaulish rulers of these tribes, such as the Aedui, gathered taxes, minted coins, regulated trade, and governed from a capital city in a way that would have been familiar to any Roman. Such states would still have seemed hopelessly backward and barbaric to a visiting Greek philosopher, but they were a far cry from the small, village-based societies of northern Gaul.

Beyond the Loire River, cutting across central Gaul, groups such as the Parisii around modern Paris and the Carnutes near Chartres maintained the older style of Celtic tribal life. Although Mediterranean imports and influences were certainly known, they did not as yet exert here the powerful influence they did in the south. Beyond these tribes, to the west in Brittany and to the north among the Belgic Gauls near the Rhine delta, trade with the south was far less common and Mediterranean civilization was barely known.

If Posidonius wanted to get a taste of the real Gaul without unduly risking his life, a good strategy would have been to establish himself in one or more Gaulish towns such as Gergovia of the Arverni or Alesia of the Aedui. In such places he was beyond the political control and restrictions of Rome but not yet beyond some semblance of civilization. There he could have stayed with and enjoyed the protection of a Greek or Roman merchant. With such a base of operations, he could have seen for himself the rich and utterly strange culture of the Celts. He could have visited nearby Gaulish villages, talked with religious and political leaders, even watched Gaulish armies facing each other in one of their never-ending wars. He could also have observed firsthand the lives of Gaulish women, joined in raucous feasts, and listened to Celtic bards sing of ancient heroes.

THE LATE first-century B.C. Greek historian Diodorus Siculus claimed that the tribes of Gaul numbered from 200,000 to 50,000 members. Even if they weren't that large, many of the tribes were certainly enormous, raising the question of how such sizable groups of warlike people were governed. Posidonius was keenly interested in political matters, so the social structure of Gaulish society would have been one of the first aspects of the culture he studied.

At the head of every Celtic tribe was a *rix*—a Gaulish word that can be translated "king" as long as we don't conjure up images of hereditary lords like Charlemagne or Henry VIII. A Gaulish king ruled over a tribe, but his power was established more by ability and influence than by birth. Kingship did tend to run in families, but the office was not automatically passed from father to son. Nephews, cousins, and even distant relatives were eligible to fill the position, as long as they were part of the nobility. Elections of some Gaulish kings seem to have been annual events, but others held the office for longer terms. Beneath the king was the warrior class, from whom the king was chosen. The warrior families owned substantial property, which allowed them the expensive weapons and horses needed for battle. Standing equal in status with the warriors were the men of special learning—Druids, bards, and highly skilled craftsmen. Beneath all these noble groups were the farm families, who made up the vast majority of the Gaulish population. Farmers were free but owed taxes and service in war to the king and nobility. At the bottom of the social order were slaves. Although the percentage of slaves in Gaulish society was probably well below that in the Greek and Roman world (where slaves could form a third of the population of a city), they were still to be found at every turn.

Aside from the fact that Gaulish kings were elected from the nobility and that they frequently served as leaders in war, little information about them has survived. We do know that the most successful were skilled politicians who shamelessly pandered to both the nobles and the commoners. As we saw in the chapter epigraph, Posidonius relates the story of Luvernius, son of King Bituis of the Arverni, who scattered riches to the crowds and held an enormous feast for his tribe in an effort to build popular support. Like a modern politician, a Gaulish king needed charisma, skill, and lots of money.

If qualities later required of an Irish Celtic king can be any guide, a Gaulish ruler also had to be an adept warrior capable of leading into battle some of the toughest and most volatile fighters the world has ever known. He had to be a man of physical perfection—loss of a limb or an eye in war was the occasion for a new king to be chosen. But he also had to be a man of wisdom and justice. It was the king's job to act as a father and protector to all his people, not just the wealthy and powerful. The health of the tribe, the fertility of its land, and the powers of nature itself depended on the just and true actions of a king. As the medieval Irish guide to kingship, the *Audacht Morainn,* states:

> It is through the king's truth that plague and great lightning bursts are kept from the people.
> It is through the king's truth that he judges great tribes and treasures.
> It is through the king's truth that beautiful children are born.

Gaulish kings also made use of an important safety valve for hot-blooded warriors and potential rivals. Mercenary service among other Gauls or in distant lands was a convenient outlet for restless and ambitious young men who might threaten the king's power if they stayed at home. Brennus and his band fighting against the Greeks for plunder in Delphi or Galatians battling Egyptians for pay beneath the pyramids—all were

Celtic warriors fighting outside their tribes in a time-honored tradition. The naked Gaesatae who fought the Romans at Telamon in Italy came from tribes in Long-Haired Gaul. These mercenaries probably consisted of disgruntled nobility and landless sons of the warrior class. It's likely their tribal kings were at the front of the crowd cheering as they marched far away from home.

AT THE CENTER of every Gaulish tribe was the fortified town of the king. For smaller tribes, this was little more than a collection of huts on a high hill surrounded by a wooden stockade. But among the larger tribes, settlements were sometimes built on low hills or at the confluence of rivers so that they could spread out over more territory. Although these large towns— called *oppida* by the Romans—did not always enjoy the natural defenses of earlier Celtic hill forts, they more than made up for any weaknesses through the elaborate defensive architecture of their walls and gates. Even a Greek traveler such as Posidonius would have been impressed as he first approached a town such as Bibracte in central Gaul. As a leading town of the Aedui tribe, Bibracte combined the natural defenses of a hill fort with the sophisticated construction of the best *oppida*. A large, steeply sided hill was the perfect setting for the town. As he approached the settlement, Posidonius would have followed ox-carts and brightly dressed Gallic warriors up to the first of a series of gates. These were open during times of peace but could create a formidable barrier if the city were under siege. The massive defensive walls of Bibracte would have discouraged even a Roman legion. A mixture of stone rubble and packed earth was interlaced with thousands of wooden beams nailed together to form a tall latticework. This was faced with more beams, planks, and finally stone. The most massive battering ram would scarcely dent such a wall, while defenders standing along the top could shower any attacking army with arrows, spears, and rocks.

Inside towns such as Bibracte lived thousands of residents engaged in trade and tribal business. The king held meetings with his warriors, celebrated feasts in the halls, and met with visiting dignitaries—such as Posidonius. Doubtless the philosopher was terrified as he approached his first Celtic king. Among eastern potentates, Posidonius knew protocol and civility were all-important, but the rough manners of a Gaulish court were completely foreign to him. The king would have sat on a raised stool surrounded by his chief warriors—all tall, fearsome-looking men with drooping mustaches and powerful physiques. The preserved heads of slain enemies would have lined the walls of the king's hall, mute witnesses to the power of the ruler. A bard stood to the side with his harp, ready to sing of the king's victories or the glories of his ancestors. A Druid or two was also close at hand, ready to advise the king on religious matters or voice concerns of his religious order in tribal affairs.

Posidonius would have stood at the side of his Greek or Roman host, who translated the philosopher's deep appreciation for being allowed to remain in the king's town and to learn the customs and history of his people. The king was probably beneficent and welcomed Posidonius to his humble settlement and tribal lands. Explore all you want, he must have said, but beware of Gaulish tempers—and do try to keep your head! Roars of laughter from the king and warriors probably followed Posidonius out of the hall. To them, he was just another foreigner who had little to offer but at least posed no threat. Wealthy Greek merchants and visiting Roman ambassadors would have rated a feast and appropriate honors, but visiting philosophers were neither rich nor dangerous enough to worry about.

POSIDONIUS undoubtedly spent a good deal of time in major towns such as Bibracte and Alesia, but the Gaulish population was overwhelmingly rural. If he wanted to learn about Celtic life in its truest forms, he would have needed to travel to the villages, farms, and forests of Gaul.

A typical Gaulish farmstead consisted of an extended family living in a small enclosure surrounded by fields and pastures. Two or three rectangular houses about thirty feet in length sat in a packed dirt compound circled by a low wall. Large wooden posts were driven deep into the ground to secure the walls of the main buildings. The timber wall frames were sometimes lined with planks but more often by thin branches covered with mud in a wattle-and-daub lattice still common in parts of the world today. A steeply pitched roof of dense thatch reached almost to the ground from a high point above the central hearth. In such a rainy climate, there were no holes in the roof to allow smoke to escape. This lack of ventilation created a constant cloud that must have sent Posidonius into a coughing fit the first time he entered a Gaulish home. But his amused hosts would have quickly explained that allowing the smoke to make its way slowly through the thatch created an insect-free area perfect for hanging and preserving meat.

When Posidonius finally grew used to the smoke, he would have seen a one-room home with an interior surrounded by a wall perhaps three feet high. On this mud wall sat dark earthenware jars full of grain and other foodstuffs, plus any implements needed for cooking. Over the ever-burning central hearth a large iron caldron hung on a chain from a rafter above. This was used for boiling large joints of meat—a Gaulish favorite. A wooden loom was a key feature of every Gaulish household. Stone weights held vertical woolen threads that were interwoven with horizontal threads to form the rough cloth of Gaulish clothing. The fabric was often dyed with bright colors to make a Gaulish family in their best clothes anything but drab. A quern for grinding grain also stood to the side, as did the sleeping platforms covered with warm animal skins. Because it was a single room, there was little privacy in a Gaulish home.

Around the main house were several outbuildings, used as workshops or to store food and animals for the winter. Livestock were free to wander the yard and were often brought inside the stockade at night to protect them from predators. The animals on a Gaulish farm was smaller than similar animals we would find today. Sheep were popular for their wool, though it was a coarser and darker variety than that of modern animals. As unappealing as such wool might be to our tastes, it was popular enough in the ancient world to be a major export item from Gaul to Italy. Pigs, who looked more like wild boars, were kept for their meat, which was also exported in a pickled form. The chickens Posidonius saw on Gaulish farms were a recent introduction from Asia via the Mediterranean. But cattle were the centerpiece of Gaulish agriculture—dark and short, they barely stood above a man's waist. They produced milk and meat, and pulled the plows that turned the rich soil. Celtic horses were quite small and used mostly for light work around the farm or for service in war. Modern films of Celtic battles would be far more accurate if they showed the Gaulish cavalry astride ponies, charging the Roman army with their feet bumping the ground.

Every farm had a few dogs to help with the sheep and cattle, as well as for hunting. The Gauls were also fond of sitting on dog skins at home and at feasts, so Posidonius would have seen many such skins drying in the sun. Gaulish fields in the autumn were ripe with wheat, barley, and millet, along with protein-rich beans of many types. Posidonius may have noticed more and more forests being cut and new fields established while he was in Gaul. The spread of new types of iron-tipped plows able to cut into tougher soils was beginning in the early first-century B.C. and was at the heart of an agricultural revolution that would soon lead to a Gaulish population explosion.

The whole of the Celtic year, including religious festivals, revolved around agriculture. The festivals are well-known from Ireland, but they must have been a major feature of Gaulish farm life as well. If Posidonius spent more than a few months in Gaul, which is likely, he could have seen these agricultural festivities in towns and farms alike. In Ireland, Imbolc took place about the first of February and celebrated the birth of spring lambs. Beltane ("bright fire" day) marked the beginning of the summer season on May 1 and was the start of open pasturage for livestock. Irish Druids drove cattle between two fires on Beltane, and Gaulish priests likely conducted similar rituals. Lughnasadh was a harvest feast honoring the great god Lugus at the beginning of August. But the chief agricultural and religious holiday of the Celtic year was held at the end of October. It was called Samain in medieval Ireland, Samonios in ancient Gaul; it is Halloween to modern revelers. It was the time of year when farms began preparing for the winter—animals were brought in from distant fields, and unneeded livestock were slaughtered for their meat. It was also a time when the world of the supernatural came closest to our own. But for the Gauls of Posidonius's day, it was mostly an occasion for feasts and well-deserved relaxation at the end of a long, hard year on the farm.

NINE

WARRIORS AND HEAD-HUNTING

*The Gauls cut off the heads of the enemies they kill in battle and hang them
around their horses' necks. Then, singing a song of victory, they take the
bloody weapons from their fallen foes and give them to their servants to carry
home. The weapons they hang on their walls like hunting trophies, but the
heads they preserve in cedar oil, storing them away carefully in chests.*

POSIDONIUS, *HISTORY*

POSIDONIUS must have thought he was well-prepared to meet
the Celtic warriors of Gaul. After all, the military might and
unparalleled bravery of the Celts were things every Greek and
Roman knew well. Posidonius had studied the Gaulish sack of
Rome, the Celtic raids on Greece and Delphi, and the Galatian
invasion and subsequent rampages through Asia Minor. He
knew that Celtic mercenaries were eagerly sought after in
Mediterranean armies, and he had probably seen more than a
few for himself as he grew up in Syria and traveled around the
Greek world.

But when Posidonius met Gaulish warriors on their home
ground and saw them fight, it was unlike anything he had ever
imagined. He had read Polybius's description of naked Celtic
warriors facing down the Romans at Telamon, and he knew the
stories of Gauls challenging Romans to single combat. He had
also heard of barbaric Celtic customs, such as decapitation and
displays of body parts as trophies, but part of him must have

believed such stories were exaggerations—or at least bizarre rituals of a distant past.

What he saw in Gaulish battles, however, was all too real to the civilized Greek philosopher. His descriptions of Celtic warfare strongly suggest that Posidonius witnessed actual battles, because the details he puts forward are too specific for secondhand stories. How was it possible that a visiting Greek could see such battles and escape to tell the tale? We have to realize that Celtic warfare—especially the type that was almost continuous between the tribes of Gaul—was not like the bloody conquests of the Romans or the devastation of modern wars. There was no destruction of whole cities, no laying waste of lands and resources, no slaughter of women and children. Celtic intertribal warfare was conducted by small groups of the nobility solely against each other. It was an affair of honor and prestige, not a wholesale massacre of innocents. It was unbelievably gruesome to a visitor from the Mediterranean, but it was limited to those of the elite classes who were born into and willingly participated in this martial way of life. No Gaulish warrior would ever dishonor himself and his tribe by attacking noncombatants or battlefield observers, such as bards, the ever-present Druids, or even visiting philosophers from Greece. The Druids in fact acted as respected referees in such battles. If too many warriors were getting killed, the Druids from both sides could step between the two armies and call an immediate halt to the fighting.

POSIDONIUS provides his readers with numerous details of Celtic warfare. One feature that must have amazed any Greek was the use of chariots in battle: "Both for travel and in war, the Gauls use a chariot pulled by two horses. This holds a driver and a warrior, who stands beside him. When they meet cavalry in battle, the warrior first throws his spears at them, then jumps off the chariot and fights with his sword." Both

Caesar and later Irish stories describe Celtic warriors so adept at chariot warfare that they could jump on the pole connecting the chariot to the horses and run along it, flinging spears in the middle of a pitched battle. Posidonius must have been stunned at the sight of chariots being used in war. For him, as for any Greek, chariot fighting was part of his heroic past. Homer sang of Greeks and Trojans driving their chariots into battle across the dusty plains of Troy, casting spears that sent the mournful souls of their enemies down to Hades. The legendary Agamemnon, Achilles, and Hector were all master charioteers, but they figured in stories from more than a thousand years in the past. For Posidonius, chariot warfare was as strange and archaic as medieval catapults and knights on horseback would be to us. But it must have been thrilling for him to watch, as if the stories of Homer he had learned as a boy were coming to life before his eyes.

Just as in the stories of the Trojan War, chariots were used by the Celts primarily for transportation in battle, not for close combat. A warrior and his driver would rush to the edge of a battle, make a great deal of noise and confusion, and fire a few volleys of deadly spears, but then the fighter would leap from the chariot and continue the fight on the ground. His charioteer would withdraw a short distance and wait until he was needed to carry home battle trophies or the warrior himself, if the battle turned against him.

The chariots were not the massive vehicles seen in cinematic epics or artistic imagination. A statue of the defiant Celtic Queen Boudicca borne in an enormous chariot pulled by gigantic steeds stands in front of Big Ben in London. But real Celtic horses would not have been able to move such a heavy chariot more than a few feet. Because Gaulish horses were small creatures, battle chariots had to be light structures of wood, otherwise the animals never would have been able to haul two men and their heavy weapons around a field of battle.

The Gaulish warriors Posidonius saw standing tall in their

chariots were men of wealth and status in their communities. Less prosperous men among the Gauls—who made up the bulk of the free population—could leave their farms and join in war as well, but only as assistants to the warrior nobility. Posidonius says it was these free men who served as charioteers. In such a secondary position, these drivers could not hope for the glory and rich spoils of war gathered by the nobility. But as clients who bravely served their wealthy patrons in battle, they could count on the crucial support of those warriors in tribal and personal affairs.

POSIDONIUS describes the dress (or lack thereof) among Gaulish warriors in great detail. It was obviously a subject that intrigued the Greek philosopher, as he knew it would his readers: "Some Celtic warriors are so unafraid of death that they go into battle wearing nothing but a small loincloth about their waist." These Gaulish fighters at least had a bit more modesty than the completely naked Gaesatae mercenaries who had fought against the Romans at Telamon more than a century before, but the addition of a loincloth provided scant protection against spears and swords. As Polybius says of the earlier Celts, fighting naked was an act of audacity designed to show contempt for their opponents. To go naked into battle was a psychological tool intended to throw the enemy off balance before the fighting even began. Posidonius, like any Greek male, was used to nakedness in the gymnasium and in athletic games. As a young man, he must have wrestled many opponents and run numerous races wearing nothing at all. But no Greek, no matter how brave, would ever have thought to face an opponent in war without heavy armor from head to foot.

However, when naked Celts are noted by classical authors, they are described as a minority on the battlefield. To fight without armor must have been a particular act of bravado that didn't appeal to most Gaulish warriors. Posidonius in fact describes the majority of such fighters as wearing beautifully colored garments: "The clothing of the Gauls is stunning. They wear long shirts dyed in various colors and pants that they call *bracae*. Around their necks they fasten cloaks flowing in stripes or decorated with checkerboard squares." The Greeks and Romans also enjoyed brightly colored clothing on occasion, but most classical battle gear was a blandly functional as modern military fatigues. To Posidonius, a fight between Celtic armies must have seemed a novel frenzy of color.

A fully outfitted Celtic warrior was an awesome sight:

> They carry shields as tall as a man, all decorated with individual designs. Some of the shields have bronze centerpieces shaped like animals that stick out from the front and serve as weapons themselves. The Gauls also wear helmets with figures on top that make the warriors look taller and even more fearsome. Some of these helmets have horns sticking out from the sides, but others have figures of animals or the fronts of birds.

Archaeologists have found such Celtic shields from Egypt to the British Isles. They were larger than Roman shields and required a strong arm to carry through a long battle, but their length gave added protection from spears and arrows. They were normally made of brightly painted wood with metal around the edges and protruding centerpieces, called bosses. Sometimes a layer of bronze was added to the face of the shield, but the extra security this gave was offset by increased weight. Most Celtic shield bosses discovered so far are simply rounded disks fixed to the fronts of the shields that stick out just a few inches. These bosses were crucial both for absorbing blows and, as Posidonius says, as instruments for pressing and smashing against an enemy in close-quarters combat. The individual decorations Posidonius describes have been amply verified by archaeologists. Beautiful examples of La Tène art, the motifs on the shields range from simple patterns of curving lines and circles to elabo-

rate representations of animals and birds. One shield from
Britain even bears the figure of a huge boar riveted to the front.

Archaeologists have also unearthed numerous Celtic helmets
from the same era, which vary in style as much as the shields.
Most are unadorned head coverings with metal flaps hanging
down over the ears—quite similar to the helmets worn by
Roman soldiers. A few feature decorations etched in the metal
or horsehair crests on top. Helmet design by necessity stressed
strength and smoothness. The last things any warrior wanted
were protrusions that would catch the edge of an opponent's
sword and knock the helmet off his head. This is why Posidonius's descriptions of horns, animals, and birds on top seems so
unlikely. One well-placed stroke of an enemy's sword would
send such an ornate helmet flying across the battlefield and
leave the warrior exposed. But again archaeology has confirmed
what Posidonius described. One Celtic helmet recovered in eastern Europe is topped by an enormous eagle with movable wings.
As the wearer raced into battle, the hinged wings would flap up
and down like those of a living bird bearing down on its prey.
As does their fighting in the nude, Celtic warriors' helmets reveal that they were sometimes more concerned with impressing
the enemy than with protecting their own bodies.

The Gauls, like other Celts from Spain to Scotland, also used
war trumpets to frighten their enemies. The Romans at Telamon were terrified by the Gaulish horns that echoed off the hills
with a deafening roar. Posidonius describes their use in
Transalpine Gaul as well: "The trumpets the Gauls use in battle
produce an incredibly harsh and barbaric sound perfectly suited
for war." Like the rebel yell in the American Civil War, the
sound of a Gaulish war horn was a powerful psychological
weapon against the enemy. Archaeologists have recovered a
number of these trumpets from many places in the Celtic world.
Unlike modern bugles, ancient Celtic horns were shaped like an
extended S that stood several feet straight above the player.
This height allowed the piercing sound to project long dis-

tances. The top of the horn was curved to the front and usually shaped in the form of an animal's head—boars and wolves were especially popular.

Posidonius describes the chain-mail shirts of Gaulish warriors, which covered their torsos from the neck to below the waist. This type of armor was probably invented by the Celts themselves during the early La Tène period and adopted later by the Romans. It was a singularly effective method of preventing penetration wounds from spears and swords. The drawbacks to chain mail are its formidable weight and the fact that it was incredibly expensive to produce, since it was made from thousands of individually forged and interlaced iron loops. The Celts were masters of metalwork, but a Gaulish blacksmith could spend weeks fashioning a single chain-mail shirt. In other words, only the wealthiest warriors could afford such protection. Most Gaulish fighters had to make do with leather jackets or their colorful tunics.

Gaulish spears were particularly impressive to Posidonius, and he comments on them at length:

> The spears the Gauls use in battle have heads of iron more than eighteen inches long and as wide as two palms placed together. Their swords are as long as the spears used by most nations—while the heads of Gaulish swords are almost as long as many swords. Some spears have straight heads, but others have a spiral shape that tears through flesh and twists into the body as it enters. Pulling out this kind of spear rips the flesh in a horrible way that makes the wound much worse.

THE ROMANS generally preferred a javelin only a few feet long that could be thrown if necessary but was more commonly used in close combat. It had only a small head and could be quickly withdrawn and used again. The enormous Celtic spears had both advantages and drawbacks. They were powerful weapons that could penetrate the toughest shields and were perfect for hurling from long distances. But these spears could be used only once—until they were pulled from an enemy's corpse—and were cumbersome in a close fight.

Gaulish swords were similarly long and elaborate. The scabbards of such weapons were beautifully decorated, as were the handles. The swords themselves were forged from the toughest iron and were several feet in length. They were ideal weapons for use on horseback or for slashing an opponent in half. However, as with Celtic spears, they were too long to allow a warrior to stab an enemy easily in a tightly packed crowd. The Roman gladius sword (from which we get the word *gladiator*) was a shorter and lighter weapon but was ideal for inflicting multiple stab wounds in tight quarters. Posidonius must have noted that when Gaulish armies all using the same weapons faced each other, there was no particular advantage to either side. But he was familiar enough with Roman gear and tactics to realize that a well-disciplined legion fighting in close quarters could methodically mow down a disorganized band of Gaulish warriors like wheat on a summer's day.

ANOTHER FEATURE of Celtic warfare that must have struck Posidonius as positively Homeric was the ritual of single combat:

> When Gaulish warriors face each other in battle, one will often come forward from his lines and challenge the best man of his opponents to fight him alone. This challenger will show off his weapons and try to strike fear in the hearts of his enemies. If someone accepts the challenge, this warrior in turn will begin boasting of his brave ancestors while he belittles his opponent—all in a mutual attempt to intimidate the other side.

When Posidonius first saw Gaulish warriors challenge each other to single combat, he undoubtedly remembered the remarkably similar contest in Homer's *Iliad* between the Greek

king Menelaus and the Trojan prince Paris. Modern readers will
also be reminded of the battle of David and Goliath in the
Bible. In fact, single combat was not unique to the ancient
Celts but was found among many early warrior cultures. It provided an unparalleled opportunity for the bravest of warriors to
take the ultimate risk—and gain the ultimate glory if they were
victorious. But there was also a clever economy that encouraged
challenges of single combat among warring tribes. If each side
in a battle were to put forward one man to represent its people,
the potential loss of men was cut from hundreds or thousands
to just one. The victors and the defeated could both walk away
from the contest without the destructive loss of life that could
critically weaken both communities. The trick, as in the *Iliad*,
was getting everyone to play by the rules. One arrow from a disgruntled Trojan in the crowd ended the single combat between
Menelaus and Paris, destroying the fragile peace and costing
countless lives in the subsequent uproar. Hot-blooded Gaulish
warriors on the losing side of a single combat challenge must
have been similarly poor sports on more than one occasion.

Single combat is again a clear sign of how the ancient Celts
viewed warfare. It was always, above all else, a contest of honor
among men, not a slaughter for territory or riches. Like the
Greeks at Troy, Gaulish fighters were only too happy to strip
their slain enemies of rich spoils—but eternal glory, being celebrated by the bards in song for generations to come, was the ultimate goal of any Celtic warrior.

Among Gaulish tribes, these rules and values were accultur-
ated into the warriors from birth. On occasion, even the Romans joined in battle with the Gauls using the same heroic
rules of conduct. In 361 B.C., only thirty years after Brennus
and his band sacked Rome, an enormous Gaul challenged the
Roman army for control of a bridge near their city: "Whoever
you Romans consider your best man, send him out to fight me!
Then we'll see which side is truly better."

Like the soldiers of King Saul before the Philistine Goliath, the Romans were reluctant to volunteer for what seemed certain death. Then Titus Manlius stepped forth and met the enemy's challenge. The historian Livy records that the Gaul was so contemptuous of this young, short Roman that he laughed, sang, danced, and finally stuck his tongue out at him—all part of the psychological warfare of single combat described by Posidonius. But Manlius had deliberately chosen a short sword for the battle, giving him an advantage over the Gaul's enormous weapon in a close struggle. At just the right moment, Manlius slipped his sword around the great Celtic shield and plunged it into his opponent's groin. The Gaulish army stood in disbelief as their champion fell to the ground. Manlius then took the golden and bloody torque from his victim and placed it around his own neck, thus gaining forevermore the nickname Torquatus—the man of the torque. The stunned Gauls withdrew and conceded the victory to the Romans.

Later Romans, however, had no interest in playing by the ancient rules of Gaulish warfare. Posidonius knew that the coming storm of the Roman army in Gaul would not pause to meet any Celtic champions in single combat. The Gauls would soon face an enemy who cared not for glory and honor in war but for victory alone.

THE ONE ASPECT of Celtic warfare that made the biggest impression on all Greeks and Romans, including Posidonius, was the gruesome practice of head-hunting—an act that had no parallel in classical battles. The historian Diodorus describes the pride the Gauls took in these trophies: "Whenever a stranger visits a Gaulish warrior's home, the host tells how his ancestors, father, or he himself had turned down offers to buy the head, arrogantly claiming that they wouldn't trade it for an equal weight of gold." Strabo, drawing even more directly on Posidonius, gives a similar account: "The Gauls practice a custom common to many northern tribes. In battle, they hang the heads of their slain enemies around the necks of their horses,

then at home they hang them on pegs in their houses. Posidonius says he frequently saw the Gauls do this and was sickened
at first but got used to it eventually."

As with single combat, Posidonius knew of Celtic head-
hunting from earlier accounts. The Roman consul Lucius Postumius was ambushed by the Gaulish Boii tribe in 216 B.C.
while riding with his army through a dense forest in northern
Italy. Postumius put up a heroic fight, but he and most of his
men were slaughtered. The Boii stripped the commander's body
of his armor and weapons, then cut off his head. At one of their
nearby temples, they carefully removed the flesh from the
consul's skull and covered it in gold. On special feast days
thereafter, they honored their noble enemy by using his gilded
head as a goblet.

Head-hunting was again not unique to the Celts. In the fifth
century B.C., Herodotus tells of Scythians in southern Russia
decapitating their enemies and using their skulls as drinking
vessels. The Scythians—eastern neighbors of the Celts—may in
fact have inspired the Gauls to take up the practice. Other
Eurasian nomads practiced similar rituals, but head-hunting
has been found throughout the world. Until recent times, some
tribesmen in New Guinea were active head-hunters. Like the
Celts, they believed that the spirit and power of an enemy
abided in his head. The head from a slain foe was not just a tro-
phy but the magical embodiment of that enemy's power. Whoever possessed such a head could draw on that warrior's courage
and spirit even after death. Thus a visitor might try to buy a
particularly potent head to use as a talisman in his own house.

Posidonius says he was sickened by head-hunting and the display of these trophies among the Gauls. In time he grew used to
the heads, but their display cannot have been something the
philosopher ever condoned. Greeks would never dream of disfig-
uring the body of even their worst enemy. In Sophocles' famous
play *Antigone*, Creon, king of Thebes, allows the body of his
traitorous nephew Polyneices to rot unburied after Polyneices

launches a war on his own hometown. But even the Theban citizens, who had every reason to hate Polyneices, were appalled by Creon's actions. The human body was sacred to the Greeks and was treated with honor. And the Romans, who thought nothing of crucifying prisoners, allowed relatives or friends to reclaim the bodies intact. But for the Gauls, to decapitate an enemy and display his head was in fact the greatest tribute that could be bestowed on a foe. A slain coward they would leave on the battlefield, but the head of a noble opponent was honored and preserved for generations.

We may be shocked at Celtic head-hunting, as were the Greeks and Romans, and wonder if such reports could have been exaggerated by those seeking to portray the Gauls as barbarians—but in truth the classical reports don't begin to compare with the gruesome evidence archaeologists have unearthed of such practices in ancient Gaul. At Roquepertuse in southern France, a Celtic sanctuary from the third century B.C. has yielded concrete evidence of severed heads used in rituals. Three pillars from the site contain niches to display human skulls, while similar temples with the skulls still in place have been found elsewhere in southern France.

These sanctuaries, however, pale in comparison with recent finds in northern France. At Ribemont and Gournay, north of Paris, archaeologists have discovered rectangular Celtic sanctuaries from around 300 B.C. that measure over ninety feet on each side. They were surrounded first by a shallow ditch, then inside by a wooden palisade. The entrance to the sanctuary was through an eastern-facing gate of three pillars with skull notches. Inside the gate at Gournay were posts with captured weapons and a open structure supported by columns. The inner temple at Ribemont covered an altar five feet square, made largely of human bones. Here the thighbones of over a thousand enemy warriors have been recovered—crushed first to expose the marrow, then burned as a sacrifice to the gods.

Just outside the walls of the sanctuary at Ribemont, archaeologists found one of the most macabre and conclusive pieces of physical evidence for Celtic head-hunting on a grand scale. The headless bodies of at least eighty warriors with their weapons were suspended there on a wooden frame several feet above the ground. These warriors had been placed on the structure as if they were still alive, holding their shields and spears for battle. It must have been a gruesome sight for any outsider to come upon: the upright corpses of dozens of fully armed, headless figures. No skulls were found with the skeletons, strongly arguing that the heads were—just as Posidonius said—preserved as trophies in Gaulish homes.

These temple discoveries help to fill in the picture of head-hunting in ancient Gaul. Once a warrior had slain an enemy and decapitated him, he took the head home for preservation. But, on at least some occasions, the headless bodies were donated to the tribal cult center, where their bones were crushed and burned in sacrifice to the gods or hung up on platforms as part of a chilling communal display. These sanctuaries were religious in function, but they also served as stark warnings to any potential enemies—if we are provoked, our warriors might be hanging your headless body here next.

TEN

WOMEN

The women of Gaul are equal to their men in size and a match for them in
strength as well. . . . They are also very beautiful.

POSIDONIUS, *HISTORY*

ONCE, long before Posidonius, there lived in eastern Europe a Celtic woman named Onomaris. We don't know exactly when she lived, but it must have been sometime soon after the great La Tène migrations of the fourth century B.C. had carried many of her people east from their alpine homeland to the lands just west of the Black Sea. Times were very hard for the Celts on the southern banks of the Danube River. The tribe of Onomaris had arrived in their new land in search of a better life but instead found only hardship and starvation. The warriors, farmers, priests, and women of the tribe appealed to their rulers to lead them to a new land where they could provide for their families. They offered to swear allegiance to anyone who would help them, but because of complacency, indecisiveness, or fear of the unknown, no man would step forward to lead them. Onomaris then rose to speak: Since no man will lead you, follow me. She must have been a remarkable woman, for in no time at all the whole tribe was behind her.

The first thing Onomaris did was reorganize the social structure of the tribe. There would be no wealthy, privileged elite. All brought forward what few goods they still possessed and placed them in a common pool for redistribution. With the efficiency and experience of a mother who had dealt with many quarreling children, Onomaris gave each family only the supply of food, animals, and weapons they needed for the journey, regardless of how much they complained. The tribe then set out north across the Danube River in search of a new home. They weren't looking for a fight—all they wanted was land on which to settle and raise their children—but they were determined to overcome anyone who stood in their way. Onomaris led the column of emigrants through forests and swamps, just as she led them in battle against hostile natives. In the end, because of the courage of this singular Celtic leader, her tribe arrived in a peaceful and prosperous land, where she ruled with strength and wisdom.

Although we possess only a few details about the life of Onomaris, she is the earliest Celtic woman we know from classical records. There could hardly be a more appropriate beginning to the long list of Celtic women who would cross the stage of history than the courageous, intelligent, and determined Onomaris. The women of the ancient Celts were not fragile souls who collapsed in tears when the world turned harsh. Again and again in Greek and Roman sources, we hear of individual women from Gaul, Galatia, and elsewhere in the Celtic world who were every bit equal—and sometimes superior—to men, in times of war and peace alike. But we have to be careful. As strong and capable as the women were, there is no evidence that ancient Celtic times were a golden age of harmony and equality between the sexes. In most places—including the Gaul of Posidonius—the culture of the early Celts was definitely a man's world, sometimes to a cruel extent. But compared with Greek and Roman women, the mothers, wives, and daughters of the Celts were accorded an enviable position of honor and responsibility.

WE'VE ALREADY SEEN the courage and cool decisiveness of two Celtic women—Chiomara and Camma of the Galatians. Chiomara was kidnapped and brutally raped by a Roman centurion but had him beheaded in revenge, placing her honor above even the objections of her husband. Camma long resisted the pleas of her family to marry her powerful and love-struck admirer, Sinorix, who had murdered her husband, Sinatus. In a plot worthy of Shakespeare, Camma chose to poison herself and the unsuspecting Sinorix just before the wedding was complete. Both these early stories, along with the ancient tale of Onomaris, give us a wonderful picture of clever, daring, and capable women that we find throughout Celtic history.

Archaeology also provides support for the idea that at least some Celtic women were powerful figures in their tribes. The previously mentioned tomb at Vix in France from about 500 B.C. contained the body of a woman in her mid-thirties adorned with fabulous riches and exotic imports from the Mediterranean. Of course, such a spectacular burial might indicate nothing more than the status of her husband—but the lady at Vix may well have been an independent ruler in her own right. She is alone in her elaborate tomb, with no comparable male graves anywhere nearby. If she were simply the consort to a powerful king, where is his grave? Her tomb lies at the foot of an important Celtic hill fort—it is quite possible she ruled there as queen and was interred in a splendid tomb by her people as a final act of honor and gratitude.

Later medieval Celtic literature can provide some guidance to the lives of ancient Celtic women, but we have to be cautious in using such evidence. The Irish stories of the Ulster Cycle speak of women who trained young warriors like the hero Cú Chulainn. They also feature Queen Medb of Connacht, who led armies and slept with any man who struck her fancy. We might imagine that this was the norm in early Ireland and perhaps then in ancient Gaul, but Irish historical records never list Medb as a queen or mention training camps for soldiers run by women. In all the Irish law texts, there is only one possible reference to a female military leader, called "she who turns back the streams of war." But this may in fact refer to an abbess or female religious figure who averts war by prayer instead of arms. Medb and the warrior women of early Irish literature are

almost certainly mythological figures, but the very fact that stories could include women as warriors indicates at least a will-
ingness on the part of the audience to consider such possibilities
and perhaps even a dim memory of a time in Celtic history
when women could fight in battle and rule over tribes.

BUT WHAT was life like for a Celtic woman who was not a
queen? Posidonius has surprisingly little to say about women in
ancient Gaul—or perhaps it's not surprising considering that
few Greek men were particularly interested in the everyday life
of any woman. For most of our information on the lives of
Celtic women, we will have to look elsewhere, but Posidonius
does provide a few notes on fashion of both genders and their
sexual behavior: "On their wrists and arms they wear bracelets.
On their necks, they wear thick gold torques. They also wear
golden finger rings and even tunics interwoven with golden
thread."

Aside from the glitter of gold on Celtic women—amply verified by archaeology—Posidonius was struck by the women's
size. The average Greek or Roman man was well short of six
feet, while the average woman was barely five feet tall. But Posidonius had the unnerving experience time and time again of
looking Celtic women in the eye or even gazing up to them. He
was also impressed by their beauty, but he claims that it was
wasted on Celtic men: "The Gaulish men prefer to have sex
with each other. They often sleep on top of animal skins surrounded by other males and roll around together on the ground.
The young men are unconcerned about proper behavior and will
offer their bodies to anyone—and they are highly offended when
anyone turns them down." We might like to know what particular experience of Posidonius prompted that observation, but suffice it to say, he witnessed homosexual behavior among the
Gauls, just as Aristotle had claimed over two centuries earlier.
How this affected relationships with women is hard to say.
Many ancient Greeks managed to combine open homosexual re-

lationships with marriage, so perhaps the same was true in Gaul.

A BETTER SOURCE on the lives of Gaulish women is Julius Caesar, who does at least comment on family life among the Celts a few decades after Posidonius. One remark he makes concerning fathers and children is perplexing: "An important difference between the Gauls and other people is that Gaulish fathers are never seen in public with their sons until they are old enough to serve as warriors. It is thought disgraceful for any father and young son to be seen together outside the home." Why a Gaulish father would be ashamed to be seen in public with a son not yet old enough to be a warrior is unknown. It may have been that the raising of children was considered strictly a woman's job and that any man who took his young son to town or even hunting in the woods was regarded as effeminate. Whatever the reason, the result was that women bore a heavy responsibility for the care of all children until the teenage years. In theory, Gaulish fathers might have been helpful and involved with their children at home, but it's hard to imagine that a society that criticized a man for spending time with a young son outside the house would encourage him to be a hands-on parent at home.

Caesar does record that the rules of Gaulish marriage show concern for the needs of women who outlive their husbands: "After a man marries, he takes the dowry he has received from his wife and matches it with an equal amount of his own money. This money is carefully invested and records are kept. Whichever of the spouses survives the other then receives the whole amount plus interest." Aside from what this says about the sophistication of the Gaulish banking system, it shows a society that sees to the needs of widows. The dowry or bride-price that a woman's family paid to a groom was not his to spend freely but had to be invested for the future needs of his wife if he died or was killed in battle.

But, as Caesar notes, life could also be very hard for a Gaulish wife: "Men have the power of life and death over their wives
and children. Also, when a man of noble birth dies, all his relatives will gather together to examine the body. If there is any
hint that the death is suspicious, they will torture and burn the
woman alive as if she were a slave." The idea that a Gaulish
man had absolute power over the lives of his family need not
have been as harsh as it sounds. Roman men also held this right
as paterfamilias over their whole households. But for a Roman
to kill his wife or child was extremely rare. Factors such as soci-
etal norms and the wife's family mitigated the actions of poten-
tially abusive husbands. In Gaul, the system was likely the
same. Although a man in theory could kill his wife with im-
punity, it's hard to imagine that many husbands would have
been willing to face the tribe and their wives' relatives to defend
such an action.

Caesar draws an interesting distinction in the second case,
when a husband died under suspicious circumstances. Among
the common people, such as farmers and craftsmen, such a
death was apparently treated simply as a tragic event. But
among the Gaulish nobility, it was an occasion for a full-scale
investigation of the wife. This is likely because, with the death
of a noble husband, a great deal of property and wealth was
at stake. If a nobleman died in war or from an obvious dis-
ease, then the wife received the previously matched and invested dowry with interest. Among noble families, this must
have amounted over time to a considerable fortune. But if the
husband's family suspected foul play, and if the family could
produce some credible evidence of the crime—to the Druids,
perhaps—the relatives could treat the widow as a murderer and
kill her in the most excruciating manner. There must have
been many a new Gaulish widow who dreaded the knock on
the door after her husband died a mysterious death. And there
must have been more than one occasion when a husband's fam-

ily, out of simple greed, manufactured evidence to implicate the wife.

WHATEVER CONSTRAINTS a Gaulish woman might have faced as a wife, it is clear that women could be powerful forces in Celtic religious life. In Chapter 14 we will see what Posidonius and others had to say about the Druids and Gaulish religion, but the role of women in Celtic religion is so fascinating that we have to consider it here. Again, we must be careful not to assume that women played a role equal with men's in Gaulish worship, but the sparse evidence we do possess clearly points to women serving in key roles. One example is a marvelous but chilling story Posidonius tells concerning a group of women living in western Gaul. As Strabo relates:

> Posidonius says that there is a small island at the mouth of the Loire River on the Atlantic coast. On that island live women of the Samnitae tribe, who are possessed by the god Dionysus and worship him in strange ceremonies and sacred rituals. No man is allowed to set foot on the island, but the women there sail once a year to the mainland to have sex with men, then return to the island. Also once each year the women tear down the roof of their temple and rebuild it before nightfall. Each woman carries a load to add to the roof, but whoever drops her burden is torn to pieces by the other women. They then carry the pieces of the dead women around the temple, shouting with Bacchanalian screams until their frenzy dies away. It is always the case that whoever drops her load has been bumped by one of the other women.

What are we to make of a passage like this? Despite Posidonius's dedication to firsthand observation, we can be sure he didn't visit the island himself or personally watch the dismemberment of the unfortunate woman. It's possible that the

philosopher traveled west in Gaul all the way to the Atlantic
Ocean—the Loire was a major trade route—but once there he
could only have gazed across the waves at the island forbidden
to men. In this case at least, he had to rely on reports from
Gauls familiar with the women and their activities. We know
from other sources, such as the Greek geographer Ptolemy, that
the Samnitae did indeed live in this area of Gaul, and modern
maps reveal several offshore islands in the area that could have
served as the headquarters of the group. It's also perfectly credible that Celtic women formed exclusive religious groups that
forbade the presence of men—even in the Greco-Roman world
there were such organizations. Posidonius says that these Gaulish women worshiped Dionysus (Bacchus to the Romans), a divinity known in the classical lands as the god of wine and
revelry. Euripides' famous play the *Bacchae* features a group of
crazed, Dionysus-worshiping women who tear King Pentheus of
Thebes limb from limb after he sneaks into one of their ceremonies. In real life, female cults of Dionysus were found in
many Greek towns, though they were better known for allowing
their members a much-needed social outlet than for serious
bloodshed.

The Celts had many gods, so it would be no surprise that
they also had a divinity who encouraged ecstatic worship. We
know from archaeology that the Gauls built wooden temples
and that many of them must have had thatch roofs, as did
Gaulish private homes, which needed replacing every year. It
must have been a lonely life for the women who tended such a
temple on a windswept island off the Atlantic coast of Gaul—
but at least it wasn't a celibate life. Once a year the women
would sail to a nearby settlement and have sexual relations with
men. Rather than imagining these women hitting the town like
sailors on leave, it might be best to consider that even the sex
may have been part of their religious life. In many ancient cultures, priestesses at certain temples acted as divine conduits for

male worshipers. To join in sexual union was an act of worship and a blessing for both parties.

But there's no escaping the shock of the seemingly unfair sacrifice of one of the women in the annual reroofing ceremony. The rebuilding of the roof each year is perfectly believable for sacred reasons as well as practical ones since many religions have similar acts of annual renewal. But how could women who lived and worshiped together so brutally murder one of their own? Again, the reality may have been different from the outside perception. Throughout history there have been a number of occasions when a member of a religious group would voluntarily sacrifice his or her life as part of worship. Among the Celts of northern Europe, there is good archaeological evidence to suggest that at least some victims of human sacrifice went willingly to their deaths as a service to the gods. Even later classical commentaries mention a human scapegoat figure among the Gauls who would voluntarily lay down his or her life for the good of the community. To believers, there could be no greater religious act than willingly to sacrifice their lives for their group and god.

The women of the Loire described by Posidonius were not the only such group of Celtic female worshipers noted in classical literature. The first-century A.D. Roman writer Pomponius Mela describes a similar cult of religious women on an island called Sena, probably off the British coast. An oracle on the island was tended by nine virgin priestesses, who were renowned for their prophecies, healing, and ability to calm storms (a useful skill in an offshore setting). Even medieval sources may retain some vague memories of earlier Celtic religious women living on sacred islands. One such story is a Welsh tale called *The Spoils of the Un-World* that describes nine virgins on an island caring for the fire beneath a supernatural caldron. This magical pot was sought after by King Arthur as a forerunner of the Holy Grail.

A story from the Roman historian Tacitus may shed some

light on what sort of Celtic oracle resided on the mysterious island of Pomponius Mela. On the east side of the Rhine River, a virgin priestess named Veleda lived among the Bructeri tribe. Even though these were traditionally German lands, many of the inhabitants were probably Celts. This is especially clear from the name Veleda, which in Gaulish means "she who sees." Veleda lived like a goddess on earth. Those who came to her seeking forecasts of the future were not allowed to lay eyes on her, as she lived in a tall tower and was approached only through relatives who acted as her priests. Even Roman colonists who lived nearby acknowledged Veleda's authority and power. Once when they were in a dispute with a local tribe, they sent gifts to Veleda and appealed to her as arbitrator. Seeing the future quite clearly, she sided with the Romans.

READING Greek and Roman sources on Celtic women is all well and good, but the best way to understand any group is to see what they say about themselves. This is particularly true in religion, as outsiders—even in modern times—inevitably present a skewed or at least inadequate view of the spiritual life of any community. Fortunately for us, a lead tablet found in 1983 near Larzac in France allows a firsthand look into the religious life of a group of Gaulish women. The text is not in Latin or Greek but in the Gaulish language itself. Much of it is obscure, but it was clearly written by women living about the year A.D. 90 who practiced secret religious ceremonies. Even though the tablet dates to the century after Posidonius and the Roman conquest of Gaul, it's almost certain such groups were present among Celtic women from much earlier times.

With a few missing pieces, the tablet begins:

Insinde se:
bnanom bricton,
eianom anuana sananderna,
brictom vidluias vidlu—— tigontias so.

Which can be tentatively translated as

> Behold:
> The magic of women,
> Their special underworld names,
> The prophecy of the seer who weaves this magic.

Even though we don't understand everything going on here, what we can read is literally spellbinding. A group of women have assembled to perform some sort of supernatural ritual. Although some Gaulish tablets mention the names of men, membership in this gathering is restricted to women alone. As in many secret societies, the members have ritual names, in this case *sananderna,* or special underworld names. This doesn't mean that the women were evil or diabolic—the Celts had no devil—just that they used these special names when calling on the gods who lived underground. Greeks and Romans also had such divinities, Hades of course being the best known, but also any number of other deities who resided within the womb of Earth herself. In charge of this group was a seer, whose title, *vidlua,* in fact comes from a Celtic word meaning "to see."

The next few lines of the tablet are very difficult to understand. It seems that the women are calling on an otherwise unknown goddess named Adsagsona to perform a binding spell. It may be that this magic is directed against two persons outside the group, perhaps former members who have left under suspicious circumstances. The exact details are all very speculative given our incomplete knowledge of the Gaulish language, but suffice it to say that the tablet is an invocation of magical power directed to a goddess of the underworld. This type of tablet was quite common in ancient times, even among the Greeks and Romans. And, as was that found at Larzac, such tablets were buried in the earth or cast in a body of water that they might better reach the gods who live beneath us.

What is especially intriguing about the Larzac tablet is how it illuminates our understanding of a later Christian poem—the famous *Breastplate* prayer of St. Patrick. The poem was not actually composed by the saint, but it is a genuinely ancient prayer for protection against the Druids and other supposedly evil forces still afoot in early Ireland. In it, the author summons the power of God to defend him against all manner of ills, including *brichtu ban,* "the magic of women." This Old Irish phrase is an exact match (given the appropriate evolution of language over time) for the corresponding words in the Larzac tablet, *bnanom bricton.* Apparently groups of women gathered together to call on the power of the gods were a feature of life not only in ancient Gaul but in early Ireland as well—and perhaps throughout the Celtic world.

THE LATE Roman author Ammianus Marcellinus wrote of Celtic women at the end of the Roman Empire and praised their abilities, not in religion but in war: "If a warrior in battle calls for help from his wife—who has piercing eyes and is far stronger than he—not even a whole troop of soldiers can stand up to them. With her neck swollen and teeth gnashing, she'll start to beat them with her enormous white arms and kick them ferociously, pounding them like a catapult."

Ammianus is obviously exaggerating to entertain his readers, but the idea that Gaulish women fought in battle shouldn't be dismissed out of hand. As we have seen, Celtic women were formidable and could deal with difficult situations. The greatest example of this ferocity is a Celtic queen from ancient Britain. Boudicca of the Iceni tribe in southeastern Britain lived more than a century after Posidonius, but her courage and intelligence make her a fitting symbol for all Celtic women.

Boudicca was born sometime in the years just before the Roman invasion of Britain in A.D. 43 under the emperor Claudius. As a young girl, she watched the southern part of her island be absorbed into the Roman Empire. The Iceni, however, had a clever king in Prasutagus—the man Boudicca was to marry. He cooperated with the Romans and was granted the status of a client ruler. This meant that his tribe remained outside Roman control as long as they supported imperial policies. The Romans made similar deals with many kings on the borders of their empire, such as the infamous Herod of Judea, because this was a practical way to guarantee their frontiers without a large and expensive commitment of troops. But these alliances were made with individual kings, not tribes, and did not automatically pass on to the client kings' heirs. As Prasutagus drew near to his death, he had the foresight to name the emperor as a joint heir with his two adolescent daughters in the hope of mollifying Roman expansionist desires after his demise. However, Rome was rarely satisfied with half of anything. When Prasutagus died, in A.D. 60, the Romans in southern Britain, who had long been gazing with envy at the rich Iceni kingdom, saw their chance. As Tacitus reports, the kingdom was looted, the nobility were robbed of their family estates, and the relatives of Prasutagus were treated like slaves. Boudicca was stripped and lashed, while her two young daughters were brutally raped.

The Romans had expected the Iceni to accept their new position as Roman subjects meekly, but they had not reckoned on Boudicca: "She was a large woman with a terrifying expression and harsh voice. Her red hair fell all the way to her hips, and she wore a huge torque of twisted gold about her neck. Her tunic was multicolored and surrounded by a thick cape fastened by a large brooch. She grasped her spear and inspired everyone around her with awe."

Boudicca quickly turned her fury into action as she roused her people and formed an alliance with the neighboring Trinovantes tribe. The Roman governor of the province, Paulinus, was occupied in western Britain, trying to subdue the Druids on the Welsh island of Anglesey, so Boudicca's timing was perfect. The first target of her army was the hated colony of Roman veterans at Colchester. As a reward for service, Roman soldiers were often granted lands in a conquered territory and settled there to farm and raise another generation of legion-naires. But the land they received was taken from natives, who were none too pleased at losing their ancestral homes and farms. Colchester was not well-guarded, as no one seriously expected an attack against a large Roman settlement. But the colonists awoke to find Boudicca's British warriors pouring over their walls and killing every Roman in sight. A few Romans made a final stand in the temple of Claudius, but they were routed within two days.

The British army then destroyed a legion of enemy troops sent to relieve Colchester and drove every Roman settler and soldier before them in panic. Boudicca's army moved on to London, which they burned to the ground, as well as St. Albans, just to the northwest. Paulinus, however, was wise enough not to meet Boudicca and her forces in battle until he had chosen a site that best suited his own army. Somewhere in central England he found the perfect spot—a narrow valley secured by a thick forest at his rear. Boudicca's warriors by now were confident they could defeat any Roman, so they moved into position in front of Paulinus. Both sides knew this was the final battle. If the British won, the Romans would be forced to leave Britain, perhaps never to return. If the Romans won, it was the end to any hope of freedom for the Celts of Britain. Not an armchair general, Boudicca rode to the front of the lines in a chariot with her daughters. After releasing a rabbit from her cloak as an augury and watching it run in a propitious direction, she reminded the army that leadership in battle by a woman was nothing new to the Britons: "I fight not as a queen of noble ancestry striving for her kingdom and lost power but as a woman of my people, enslaved, brutalized by the whip, tortured by the violation of my daughters. . . . Understand this—you must win here or die trying! You men can live and be slaves if you want, but my purpose as a woman is victory!"

The final battle against the Romans was not a heroic contest

for honor or glory, as were most Celtic wars. It was a simple
fight for survival as a free people. The British fought with ut-
most bravery, but in the end they were defeated by the superior
discipline of the Roman army. Tacitus reports that eighty thousand British died, with no mercy given to the women. Boudicca,
in a final act of defiance, killed herself before the Romans could
reach her.

ELEVEN

FEASTING

Posidonius says that in ancient times, when whole joints of meat were served at feasts, the best man at the table would get the thigh. But if someone else claimed it, they would fight to the death.

ATHENAEUS, *DEIPNOSOPHISTAE*

WE HAVE more information from Posidonius on feasting than we do on almost any other aspect of Celtic society. It may seem strange that eating habits feature so prominently in the writing of a Greek philosopher, but this is thanks both to how Posidonius's writings were preserved by later authors and to the great importance of feasting as a social ritual among the Gauls.

One of the three primary writers of antiquity who quoted or paraphrased Posidonius at length was an Egyptian named Athenaeus, who lived about A.D. 200. Athenaeus wrote a book called the *Deipnosophistae* (The Educated Banquet), the setting of which is an elaborate dinner party of intellectuals who for several days discuss every subject under the sun, but especially dining habits of people around the Mediterranean world. Posidonius was obviously a favorite of Athenaeus, as he quotes the philosopher's detailed observations on Celtic feasting several times. But why did Posidonius himself bother to record such supposedly mundane events? Because, in short, feasting among the ancient Celts was much more than eating—it was court ceremonial, social one-upmanship, and barroom brawl, all rolled into one.

To understand Celtic feasts, we have to remember that the nobles of a tribe were held together above all by bonds of honor and status. Tribal leaders ruled largely through personal influence and patronage, honoring those warriors who fought bravely in battle with gifts—and, more important, social recognition. It was at feasts that this recognition was given by the king and other noble hosts. Who received the best seat at a meal and was honored with the choicest cut of meat was vital to the Gaulish nobility in a way that is hard for us to imagine. Any perceived slight by a host or another warrior was sufficient reason for ferocious argument and even bloodshed.

One way to appreciate the importance of Gaulish feasting is to see how it worked in a similar Celtic culture, that of medieval Ireland. A wonderful early tale called *The Story of Mac Dá Thó's Pig* tells a group of belligerent Irish warriors from different tribes who came together and demanded that they be given an amazing hound. Their tribe, each side claimed, was the noblest in all the land and thus deserved such a gift. The nervous owner of the hound invited both parties to an elaborate feast featuring a pig so large it was pulled on a cart by sixty oxen. It was boiled in an enormous pot, into which everyone was expected to plunge his hooked spit at the proper time. When the dinner was ready, there was immediate contention about who should receive the first and finest portion of meat. A boasting contest ensued, in which each side insulted the other in the coarsest of ways while threatening bloody mayhem. Finally, a warrior named Cet seemed to gain the upper hand and was ready to dig in when an opposing fighter named Conall walked into the room and told him to get away from the pig. Cet—after a nasty exchange of insults—finally conceded that Conall was the better man but said that if his brother Anlúan were there, he would teach Conall a lesson: "Oh, but he is here, said Conall. He then took Anlúan's head out of his bag and threw the bloody mess on Cet's lap." The feast dissolved into a riot as each side fought and slew their opponents—even the hound was killed in the end. The story is exaggerated fiction, of course, but it is based on a very real heroic ethos that dominated the warrior cultures of both ancient Gaul and medieval Ireland. And it was an ethos that Posidonius experienced first-hand.

ARCHAEOLOGY AND PLATO both confirm that the ancient Celts loved wine—and we have seen how a group of the fourth-century B.C. Celts organized a banquet to lure their Illyrian foes into a death trap. But the earliest extensive description of Celtic feasting comes from an Athenian named Phylarchus, writing in the third century B.C. This Greek author says that the Celts of his day would place large portions of bread and boiled meat on their tables. But, he emphasizes, no one would dare begin eating until they saw their leader take up his portion first.

Phylarchus also passes on a wonderful story of an incredible feast sponsored by a wealthy Celt named Ariamnes. This bene-factor was not content with throwing a single dinner party but instead organized an elaborate simultaneous banquet spread throughout his territory:

> Ariamnes announced one day that he would give a yearlong feast for all his countrymen—and this is how he did it. He di-vided the land into sections, all marked out at suitable dis-tances along the roads. At every station, he built a feasting hall out of poles, straw, and wicker that held four hundred men or more, depending on how large the nearby towns were. In these halls were enormous caldrons with every kind of cooked meat (the caldrons had been specially made the year before). Ariamnes then provided oxen, pigs, sheep, and every other kind of meat daily for the feasts, along with countless jars of wine and loaves of bread.

PHYLARCHUS says that not only were the Celts of nearby towns invited to the daily banquets but even strangers who hap-pened by were welcomed. Ariamnes may have provided this yearlong bounty solely because of his kind heart, but a better explanation is that he was trying to win popular support as a leader. Like the Roman emperors who gained the loyalty of the mob with bread and circuses, Ariamnes knew the surest route to any Celt's heart was through his stomach.

TWO HUNDRED years later, the descriptions of Celtic feasts given by Posidonius are remarkably similar but much more detailed. His account makes it abundantly clear that he was present as a guest at these banquets. As with single combat, when Posidonius first walked into a Celtic feasting hall, he must have felt he had stepped back in time a thousand years, to the days of the Homeric heroes:

> The Celts feast while sitting on dry grass in front of wooden tables raised just off the ground. They eat only small portions of bread but enormous portions of meat—either boiled or cooked on spits over an open fire. They eat like lions but in a surprisingly clean manner. They take the whole cooked joint of an animal in their hands while they eat, though sometimes they will cut off a piece with a small knife they keep in its own sheath on their sword.

We can imagine Posidonius seated in a large wicker-and-wood hut of a local chieftain at one of these feasts. He was probably accompanied by a translator, who helped him converse with the other diners and adapt to the customs of Celtic feasting. His host would have welcomed him to the banquet and introduced him to the other guests—men, of course, and probably warriors as well. He would undoubtedly have been pleased to have such an unusual guest at his dinner, even though the visitor would surely have seemed as strange to the Gauls as they did to him. They had seen Greek and Roman businessmen before, but sophisticated travelers like Posidonius rarely ventured so far from the civilized Mediterranean world. For Posidonius, in turn, Gaulish feasts were a new experience. Banquets back in Athens or Rhodes were occasions of cultured dining and philosophical discussion as guests reclined on couches. But here he was, in the middle of barbarian Gaul, sitting on the ground in a smoky hut eating huge chunks of meat while giant warriors bellowed and decapitated heads looked down on him from the walls.

One thing that Posidonius noticed immediately about his fellow guests was the peculiar way they used their mustaches at meals. By this point he was perfectly accustomed to the long, thick mustaches of the Gaulish warrior aristocracy. They had struck him as just another odd custom of the upper-class Celts, especially as he notes that the poorer men were normally clean-shaven or wore only short beards. But the noblemen had the peculiar habit of drinking their wine and thick beer deliberately through their bushy mustaches, using their ample facial hair to strain the dregs out of their beverages.

Posidonius paid careful attention at these dinners and records in detail the arrangement of the guests:

> Whenever the Celts hold a feast, they sit in a circle with the most powerful man at the center, like the chorus leader in a Greek play. His power may be because of his bravery in war, noble birth, or simply his wealth. Next to him sits the host of the feast, followed in order on both sides by the other guests in descending rank. Behind each guests stands his shield bearer, while the lesser warriors sit apart in their own circle.

POSIDONIUS says that wine imported from Massalia was served at the finest feasts. Roman merchants were especially active in the wine trade, bringing huge jars up from the Mediterranean by river and road. In exchange for each jar of wine, the Gauls would give the merchants one slave—an extravagant payment by ancient standards that made the Gaulish wine trade a lucrative business.

Greek diners would elect a banquet leader, who determined how much water was to be mixed with the wine—the more

water, the more serious the discussion. But the Gauls shocked
Posidonius by rarely mixing water into their wine. He also observed that at the feasts of less wealthy Gauls, a honey-flavored
beer called *corma* was a favorite beverage. The beer was poured
into a huge cup and passed around the circle. A guest was expected to take short but frequent sips as the drink made its continuous rounds. But Posidonius had to be careful because, he
says, the cup was always passed to the right. To hand it to the
left was to offend the Celtic gods. The Romans had a similar
preference for the right—in fact, the Latin word for "left" is *sin-
ister.*

WHAT PARTICULARLY struck Posidonius about Gaulish feasts
was the violence always simmering beneath the surface—a violence that often erupted into bloodshed, as Athenaeus relates:
"Posidonius says in the twenty-third book of his *History* that
the Celts often engage in single combat at their feasts. This
usually begins as a friendly contest with the warriors striking
each other in good fun. But sometimes blood is spilled, tempers
get out of control, and the two combatants will try to kill each
other, unless their friends step in and separate them."

The combination of strong drink and bravado is dangerous in
any culture, but among the raging egos of Gaulish warriors, it
could be deadly. Posidonius watched two giant Gaulish warriors
red-faced with Massalian wine draw their swords in what was at
first a friendly contest. The dinner guests all cheered for their
man as the two fighters circled each other, each deriding the
other's alleged bravery, manhood, and mother's virtue. A few
halfhearted blows landed on shields at first, then thrusts and
jabs began with increasing vigor. Soon the banter was replaced
by grim determination to humiliate the opponent and avoid losing even a mock battle in front of friends. A quick stab drew
blood from the rival's arm, then a counterthrust had both men
bleeding. A few in the crowd called for an end, gallantly proclaiming that both men were worthy fighters—but it was too

late. The mixture of wine and pride was unstoppable as the warriors began to fight as if on a battlefield. Platters of food were overturned, and feasters, including Posidonius, scrambled to get out of the way. The long Celtic swords cut through the air again and again, until one of the drunken warriors made the fatal mistake of lowering his shield for only a moment.

As they carried the dead warrior off, Posidonius must have been horrified. Everything he had heard about the barbarous Celts was surely true. One of the other guests must have noticed the pale and shaking philosopher, offering him a cup of wine to calm his nerves. This is nothing, the Gaul must have said, as he then told Posidonius a story of the old days, when feasts were *really* wild: "Posidonius says that in ancient times, the bravest man at a feast would claim the thigh, the choicest portion, from the pot. If anyone rose to challenge him, the two would fight to the death." The phrase *in ancient times* is the key. It's safe to say that in this fragment Posidonius passes on a snippet of an old Gaulish myth amazingly similar to the medieval Irish tale of Mac Dá Thó's Pig. We have only Posidonius's brief summary, but the passage has all the marks of a heroic tale told by a bard around the hearth fire.

The next fragment, however, is even more intriguing: "In former days, men would gather pledges of silver, gold, or sometimes jars of wine from those at a feast. They would then divide these promised gifts among their relatives and friends. Finally, they would stretch out on their backs on top of their shields and someone would cut off their head." Again, Posidonius is clearly relating a tale from the old days; he never claims to have witnessed such an event himself. It's possible that such public suicides could have occurred in ancient Gaul. The recurring elements of reckless bravado, public spectacle, and decapitation seen so frequently in Celtic culture are all present. But whether these events had actually happened or not, they had entered Celtic folklore and were passed on to Posidonius. One feature that makes the tale so compelling is its similarity to later Celtic and Celtic-inspired stories.

In an Old Irish tale called *Bricriu's Feast,* a huge, ugly man one day approached the great Ulster heroes as they were sitting at a banquet. The man offered an interesting challenge to the warriors—he would allow them to cut off his head if the next night he might cut off theirs. The men laughed, and one named Fat Neck agreed to the bargain, thinking the stranger to be a fool. Fat Neck cut off the visitor's head with one stroke, but the stranger then picked up his head and walked out of the hall. Suddenly all the warriors realized their foolishness—and Fat Neck immediately backed out of the deal. But young Cú Chulainn berated his fellow warriors and reminded them that a man is only as good as his word. When the stranger returned, Cú Chulainn agreed to the bargain himself, chopped off the stranger's head again, and laid his own neck on the block the following night. The stranger raised his ax and brought it down but only nicked Cú Chulainn's neck. He then revealed himself as an Irish god and rewarded Cú Chulainn for his integrity.

Readers familiar with the famous tale *Sir Gawain and the Green Knight* will recognize a similar plot; the medieval English story is borrowed from the earlier Irish narrative. But in truth the Irish story is almost certainly an adaptation of a widespread pre-Christian Celtic tale, a variant of which was first heard by Posidonius at a feast in ancient Gaul.

TWELVE

BARDS

The Celts have singing poets called bards who play an instrument much like
a Greek lyre. These bards sing both praise songs and satire.

POSIDONIUS, *HISTORY*

In the ancient Celtic world, a poet was the modern equivalent of
rock star, academic historian, and political commentator all
rolled into one. The range and power of a poet in such a traditional society may be hard for us to imagine, but we have to remember that the ancient Gaul of Posidonius was primarily an
oral culture. It was, moreover, a society where the leading members—especially the kings and warriors—were desperately hungry for respect and praise. This was provided by the Celtic bard,
who sang songs of their wondrous ancestors, the gods and history of the tribe, and the warriors' own generosity and un-
matched bravery in battle. The praise of a bard was the measure
and means of respect in a world where honor was everything.
Without the songs of a bard, there was no way to achieve what
the Greek heroes of Homer's epics also most craved—everlasting
glory.

But praise did not come cheap. A Celtic bard was a professional who expected to be well-paid for his services. Woe be to
the Gaulish king who was miserly in compensating a poet for
his song, for the verses of praise could quickly turn to biting
satire. One of the earliest stories we have of a Celtic bard comes
from a fragment of Posidonius—the previously mentioned passage of the Gaulish leader Luvernius, who attempted to woo

supporters among his Avernian tribesmen with his overflowing generosity:

> Luvernius rode through the fields on his chariot, handing out gold and silver to all the Gauls to increase his own popularity. He also set up a huge feast in an enclosure over a mile wide, so that anyone could come and enjoy the expensive wine and abundant food he provided, all served by his own attendants. On the last day of the feast, Luvernius was driving away just as a poet arrived. The bard ran along beside Luvernius, singing of his generosity and lamenting his own late arrival. Luvernius was so delighted by the song that he threw the bard a bag of gold. The poet then picked up the gold from behind the chariot and composed another song, this time celebrating the fact that even the tracks of Luvernius's chariot produced rich benefits for all.

Luvernius was a very wise politician. If he had ignored the tardy poet, the bard would have just as quickly composed a stinging satire against the ruler, lambasting his miserliness and mocking his expensive public relations campaign.

WE CAN SEE something of the Celtic poet's status and power from looking at the life of a bard in the closely similar world of medieval Ireland. There the highest rank of poets had the same honor price as a king—that is, any injury to such a bard required the same compensation paid to the head of a tribe. Irish bards were said to have supernatural powers, so that a particularly powerful satire could even kill its victim. Before we dismiss this as exaggeration, consider the force of shame in a society where "face" was everything—to endure the full, public wrath of a bard and the taunts of those who repeated his song might drive anyone into despair, sickness, or even suicide.

Irish poets came to such an influential position in society by years of study under a master poet and by a touch of divine inspiration. The famous Irish warrior Finn was also a poet; he learned the art of poetry as a boy from a master bard named Finnéces, who lived by the Boyne River north of Dublin. Finnéces had been waiting seven years by a pool on the Boyne to catch a magical salmon of wisdom. There was a prophecy that whoever first ate of the salmon would gain its power for himself. Finnéces finally caught the salmon one day but was so tired from the effort that he gave it to young Finn to cook for him—along with a stern warning not to taste the fish. Finn brought the salmon to his master after it was prepared and swore he had not eaten any for himself. However, the boy confessed that he did burn his thumb when he touched the fish and then quickly stuck his thumb in his mouth. Finnéces realized that he had lost the magical power of the salmon to Finn. Thereafter, whenever Finn needed wisdom—poetic or otherwise—all he had to do was suck his thumb.

Not every would-be Irish poet learned his art through a chance encounter with a fish. It seems that some were destined by fate or the gods to rise to greatness. As in many such stories around the world, the young Irish boy Amairgen showed little promise of greatness as a child. Amairgen was in fact mute and hideously ugly until he reached his early teens. One day when his household was visited by a servant of a great bard, Amairgen suddenly blurted out a perfectly formed line of poetry. When the poet heard this, he realized the boy would be a threat to his own standing and at first tried to kill him but eventually adopted Amairgen, who went on to become the chief poet of northern Ireland.

Finn and Amairgen are mythological figures, but even real poets in early Ireland had supernatural means to increase their skill. One of the most famous was a ritual known as the *imbas forosnai*, or the "illumination of wisdom." In order to perform this ceremony, the poet had first to chew the raw flesh of a pig, dog, or cat. He then placed a stone by his door, chanted a hymn to the old gods, and lay down to sleep for several days with his palms pressed against his cheeks. At the end of his rest, he hoped to be granted a vision from the supernatural world.

Even after St. Patrick and the acceptance of Christianity in Ireland, the bards held positions of undiminished influence. Some clergy complained of their thinly veiled pagan rituals but were helpless to stop a tradition so deeply rooted in Ireland's Celtic heritage. The priests must have been especially displeased to see the occasional woman among the ranks of the Irish poets, as early Irish laws and tales both mention female bards.

POSIDONIUS surely spent many nights listening to Gaulish bards as they sang their songs around the hearth fires of kings and warriors. He notes that the wealthiest of Celtic chiefs had their own full-time poets, whom he calls *parasites*—a Greek word meaning "dining companion." These bards were always at hand, especially at dinners, to regale the king's guests with songs of their patron's glory.

But for poets to work their magic, they need most of all a willing and eager audience. That the Gauls were active consumers of bardic songs and greatly honored poetry is best seen through a wonderful story of a later Greek visitor to Gaul named Lucian. In the second century A.D., two hundred years after Posidonius, Lucian traveled to Gaul as an itinerant lecturer on literature and philosophy. The Romans by this time had long controlled Gaul, but the Celtic love of poetry was still very much alive, as Lucian discovered. In between lectures, the Greek traveler whiled away his time visiting Gaulish temples. On one sightseeing excursion, he wandered into a temple of Hercules but was confused and troubled by what he saw:

> The Celts call our god Hercules by the name Ogmios in their
> native tongue—and their images of him are not at all like our
> own. In their pictures, he is an old, bald man with only a few

gray hairs left on the back of his head. He is wrinkled and dark like an ancient sailor—you would think you were looking at an image of the underworld ferryman Charon or the Titan Iapetus in Hades. But in spite of how he looks, he has all the usual equipment you would expect to see with Hercules—lion skin over his shoulder, club in his right hand, arrows and bow in his left.

LUCIAN couldn't believe his eyes. The greatest Greek hero—a son of Zeus—honored and worshiped throughout the Mediterranean world, was in Gaul portrayed as a ragged old man.

Lucian continues: "At first I thought the Gauls were making fun of glorious Hercules to spite the Greeks, since the story goes that the hero had once stolen cattle from their lands while he was chasing the monster Geryon through western Europe." This was a tale every Greek and Roman schoolboy knew. Before eventually becoming a god himself, Hercules underwent many trials, including the famous twelve labors. Number ten on this list was a journey to the far west to find the three-bodied monster Geryon and steal his cattle—all of which, according to legend, Hercules managed nicely with a maximum of slaughter and general troublemaking for the local inhabitants.

Lucian's anger then turns to confusion as he looks at the rest of the image:

I haven't mentioned the oddest part yet—this old Hercules drags behind him a group of men all chained by their ears! The chain itself is a thin and delicate work of gold and amber, like a beautiful necklace. The bound men could easily escape such a weak chain if they wished, but they all follow Hercules gladly, almost stepping on his feet just to be near him. I suppose they would even be upset if they were freed. Odder still is how the painter attached the chain to Hercules—since he has his hands full with his club and bow, the end of the chain is fixed to the tip of his tongue. He even turns to his captives and smiles.

Parthenon temple on the Acropolis of Athens, the city where Posidonius studied philosophy. (*Philip Freeman*)

Valley of Hallstatt in western Austria, site of early archaeological evidence of the Celts. (*Philip Freeman*)

Hochdorf couch from sixth-century B.C. Celtic royal grave near Stuttgart, Germany. (*Württembergisches Landesmuseum Stuttgart*)

Hochdorf tomb caldron with lions on rim. (*Württembergisches Landesmuseum Stuttgart*)

Reconstructed Celtic warrior's grave from Austria. (*Philip Freeman*)

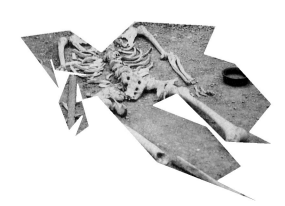

Basse-Yutz flagon from France, c. 400 B.C. (© *The Trustees of the British Museum*)

Pillars with notches for severed heads from a Gaulish sanctuary at Roquepertuse in southern France. (*Musée de la Vieille Charité, Marseille, France/Bridgeman Art Library*)

Fibulae from the La Tène period. The Celts used these elaborately decorated pins to fasten their cloaks. (*Kelten Museum, Hallein, Austria*)

Handle of an early Celtic flagon, c. 400 B.C. (*Kelten Museum, Hallein, Austria*)

Etruscan horseman fighting a naked Celtic warrior, fifth-century B.C.
monument from Bologna, Italy. (*Philip Freeman*)

Reconstructed interior of an early Celtic home. (*Kelten Museum, Hallein,
Austria*)

Dying Gaul.
(Capitoline Museum, Rome)

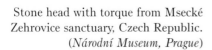

Battersea Shield from London,
England. (© *The Trustees of the
British Museum*)

Stone head with torque from Msecké
Zehrovice sanctuary, Czech Republic.
(Národní Museum, Prague)

Gundestrup caldron. Although probably Thracian in origin, this large caldron is decorated with many images from Celtic religion and mythology. (*National Museum of Denmark*)

Statue of the Celtic horse goddess Epona. (*André Rabeisen, Alesia Museum*)

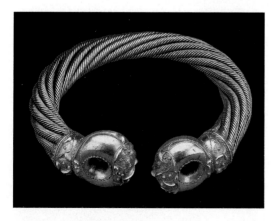

The Great Torque from Snettisham, England, early first century B.C. (© *The Trustees of the British Museum*)

Body of Lindow Man from Cheshire, England, first century A.D. (© *The Trustees of the British Museum*)

Book of Kells, Trinity College, Dublin. The elaborately decorated Book of Kells continued the traditions of early Celtic La Tène art into Christian times. (*The Board of Trinity College, Dublin*)

Archaeologists have found plenty of Roman slave chains, but all have thick iron neck rings and heavy links. Captives literally stooped from the weight as they walked, hands bound, and had no chance of escaping such fetters. Thus Lucian was totally baffled by the image he saw in the Gaulish temple:

> I stood for a long time before the painting, full of anger, perplexity, and wonder. Finally a nearby Celt came up to me. He was a well-educated man who spoke excellent Greek but also knew the local traditions well. "You seem puzzled and disturbed by the image," he said, "but I can explain it to you if you'd like. We Gauls disagree with you Greeks that Hermes is the god of eloquence. We think that the power of the spoken word is best represented by Hercules, since he is much stronger. And don't be shocked that we portray him as an old man, for the true power of eloquence comes in the ripeness of years, not with youth. . . . So it makes perfect sense that you see Hercules here leading men away by his tongue. . . . The common tradition of Gaul is that Hercules achieved his greatest triumphs by the power of his words."

The narrative of Lucian is one of the best stories we have of the bardic tradition first seen in Posidonius and later found in medieval Celtic literature. We know from inscriptions that the Gauls did indeed have a god named Ogmios, who may be the same as Ogma, a later Irish god and hero. Ogma was in fact known in Irish by the Herculean title *trénfer* (the strong man) and was said to be the inventor of writing. Even if the connection between the Gaulish and the Irish gods is uncertain, Lucian's short tale is a marvelous example of the ancient Celtic respect for the spoken word—and the eloquent power of Gaulish bards.

THIRTEEN

GODS

The chief god of the Gaulish people is Mercury—there are images of him
everywhere. They say he is the inventor of all arts and the guide
for every journey.

JULIUS CAESAR, *GALLIC WAR*

THE GREEKS and the Romans worshiped an impressive number of gods. Some divinities guarded hearth and home, while others took care of agriculture, war, love, or a thousand other aspects of life. To most modern monotheists, this seems like an untidy and unnecessarily complicated arrangement of the universe—but people in ancient times looked at life quite differently. To them, the world was a very big and often dangerous place. Knowing that there was a whole host of gods watching over you could be a great comfort. If, for example, you were worried about your sickly olive trees or the birth of your first child, there was a god who took care of just this problem. You sacrificed a young goat to the appropriate divinity, and you were all set. A few people in the ancient Mediterranean world, like the Jews, advocated a single divine being, but to the majority of everyday Greeks and Romans, this seemed ridiculous. How could one god be everywhere at once, watching over everything? Better to worship a local god who was paying close attention to your particular barley field than a universal God who had a million other things on his mind.

The Celts shared this polytheistic view of the world with the Greeks and Romans. To the Gauls, Celtiberians, and every other ancient branch of the Celtic family, from Asia Minor to

Ireland, the land, waters, and sky were populated by a vast array of gods. Unfortunately, the evidence we have for these gods is limited to a few references in the writings of classical authors, along with a handful of puzzling inscriptions. And with the Greek and Roman writers, we again face the problem of interpretation, since we are forced to look at the ancient Celts through the eyes of a people who were often hostile toward them. Even those who were sympathetic naturally enough present their evidence of Celtic religion from their own points of view. A Roman writing about Celtic gods, for example, would always find similarities to his own religious system to explain something so new and strange. A Gaulish god of war would seem most like Mars, a healing god would be called Apollo, and so forth. Differences would be overlooked in favor of similarities, both to aid the classical writer's own understanding of Celtic religion and to help explain Celtic gods to his readers.

In the end, trying to understand Celtic religion will always be an exercise in frustration if we expect answers to all our questions. It's very much as if some future age would try to reconstruct the whole of Christianity based solely on a church newsletter and a few casual remarks from non-Christian writers. But if instead we approach Celtic religion with humility, realizing our limitations and carefully weighing the surviving sources, we can at least see the outline of a world filled with gods.

THE EARLIEST classical author to mention Celtic gods is the Greek historian Timaeus, who briefly describes two divinities in the early third century B.C.: "The Celts who live on the shore of the Atlantic Ocean honor the Dioscuri above all other gods. There is an ancient tradition among them that these two gods came to them from the sea." This short statement is typical of classical descriptions of Celtic religion, as it leaves us with so many questions. The Atlantic shore of Gaul is a big place. Were these gods worshiped by Celts all along its length or just locally? We know that the Greek Dioscuri (literally "sons of Zeus") were the twin gods Castor and Pollux, but what were their Celtic names? Aside from their origin in the sea, what is the rest of the myth surrounding them? How were they worshiped? In spite of our questions, we should be grateful to have a fragment of a Celtic myth preserved from such an early date— for even in the third century B.C., it is described as ancient. What we can know for certain is that somewhere along the western coast of Gaul a little after the year 400 B.C., a group of Celts were worshiping twin male gods above all other deities. These brothers, as they told the story, arose one day from the ocean. It's no surprise that Timaeus would identify them with Castor and Pollux, as these siblings were often identified with the sea and were prominent not only in Greek but in early Roman worship. Twin gods are also found throughout the world—from the ancient Germans to the Maya of Central America—and are often associated with creation stories.

Another third-century B.C. Greek author, named Eudoxus, mentions a peculiar Celtic invocation ritual: "When locusts invade the land of the Celts and threaten their crops, they offer prayers and sacrifices to call forth birds. The birds hear these pleas and come in flocks to eat the locusts. If anyone captures one of these birds, he is sentenced to death. If the offender is pardoned, the birds become angry and will not return if called on again." Strictly speaking, the Celts in this ritual prayed to birds rather than to the gods, but the line between the two could sometimes be fuzzy in the ancient world. In many early societies, including the Greeks' and Romans', the birds of the sky were seen as intermediaries between the worlds of gods and humans. The appearance or movement of birds was carefully studied by respected diviners, who wished to know the will of the gods. In medieval Celtic stories, gods often take the form of birds, shifting between human and avian forms at will. The Irish hero Cú Chulainn foolishly attacked a flock of supernatu-

ral birds in one early tale, only to have two goddesses beat him
senseless with horsewhips and leave him bedridden for a year.

A second report of Celtic bird magic comes from the geographer Artemidorus of Ephesus in the following century: "There
is a certain harbor on the coast of Gaul named Two Crows. In
this place are two crows whose right wings are white. If anyone
has a dispute, each person places barley cakes on a raised piece
of wood. The crows will then fly to the cakes, eating some but
scattering others. Whoever has his barley cakes scattered is
judged the winner of the dispute." White is always the color of
the supernatural in Celtic mythology, so it's no surprise that
these two crows are marked as messengers of the gods by their
white wings. Although many uncertainties remain, we at least
know from these two passages that some Celts in the centuries
before Posidonius were calling on the gods and their winged intermediaries both for protection from the ravages of nature and
as judges in disputes.

Later in the same passage, Artemidorus makes a brief but
tantalizing reference to the worship of two Celtic goddesses:
"There is an island near Britain on which sacrifices are performed for Demeter and Core, just as they are on Samothrace."
Is this the same island off the British coast mentioned by Pomponius Mela as the home of the nine prophetic virgins? Could
Artemidorus even be referring to Ireland? Being a typical Greek
writer, he identifies these two divine figures with goddesses
from his own pantheon. Demeter was the protector of grain and
harvests, a divine figure who sustained the human race. She was
one of the most ancient Greek gods, with clear parallels to cult
figures in Mesopotamia and Egypt. Her daughter, Persephone
(known also as Core, "the girl"), was violently abducted by
Hades and carried to the underworld. Persephone was forced to
spend the cold winter months beneath the earth but returned to
the upper world each year with the flowers of spring. Both were
worshiped as symbols of fertility and rebirth throughout the

Greek world, including the Greek island of Samothrace, in the northern Aegean Sea. Demeter was especially tied to ancient mystery religions that promised immortality and renewal after death, just as plants and crops return to life each spring. We could speculate endlessly on how the Celts worshiped these two goddesses, but our facts are too limited for any but the barest conjectures. What we do know is that some Celts in the second century B.C. were worshiping a pair of female divinities on an island near Britain. These two goddesses were a mother and daughter who—if they were anything like their classical counterparts—were concerned with both the fertility of the land and the human hope for life after death. Because, in Celtic myth, western islands are often connected with the supernatural, death, and rebirth, we might even speculate that this particular island was a religious site visited by early Celtic pilgrims seeking assurance of personal immortality.

POSIDONIUS has a great deal to say about Druids and Celtic religion but little about the actual gods of Gaul. He does mention, as we saw earlier, the frenzied women near the Loire River who worship a god like the Greek Dionysus, but he offers no list of Celtic deities or descriptions of their powers. But to our good fortune, we do have just such a list from none other than Julius Caesar. The conqueror of Gaul was surprisingly interested in the religion of the people he defeated—perhaps as a result of his service as a priest in Rome. In any case, his short description of the Gaulish pantheon is the most detailed account of the Celtic gods we possesses:

> The chief god of the Gaulish people is Mercury—there are im-
> ages of him everywhere. They say he is the inventor of all arts
> and a guide for every journey. He is also the protector of trade
> and business. After Mercury, they worship Apollo, Mars,
> Jupiter, and Minerva. These gods are in charge of the same
> areas of life as among other people. Apollo heals diseases,

Minerva is in charge of handicrafts, Jupiter rules over the sky,
and Mars is in charge of war.

Our challenge two thousand years later is to look carefully at
this passage and try to understand the identity and role of these
Gaulish gods using every tool we can muster, such as other classical references, archaeology, and—with suitable caution—later
Celtic mythology from Ireland and Wales.

The first god on Caesar's list is the easiest to identify but
also the most surprising in his attributes. We have already seen
that Lugus, the god of arts, was worshiped among the Celtiberians and Irish. There is little doubt that the Gaulish god Caesar
calls Mercury was this same Lugus—but he must have been
something of a shock to Roman readers. Mercury (Hermes to
the Greeks) was an important but decidedly second-rank god in
the classical pantheon, far below the chief god, Jupiter (Greek
Zeus). Mercury's primary role was messenger boy for Jupiter,
bearing dispatches from the Olympian throne to gods and mor-
tals alike. He also served the Greeks and Romans as a guide on
journeys, as a divine patron of commerce and business, and as
the god of thieves. While Caesar emphasizes that Gaulish Lugus
was also a guide for travelers, his role as a master of arts is the
quality most strongly reflected in later Celtic stories.

In early Irish mythology, the equivalent god Lug is known as
samildánach (possessing all skills), a description quite similar to
Caesar's Mercury. In one Irish tale, Lug approaches the court of
the divine king Nuada of the Tuatha Dé Danann, later known
as the fairy folk. The gods are all feasting at the royal hall of
Tara when Lug asks permission to enter. The gatekeeper tells
him only someone with a needed skill can enter while the feast
is in progress. Lug replies that he is a skilled smith, but the
gatekeeper says they already have one. I'm also a poet, a harper,
a physician, and master of many other crafts, Lug offers. Sorry,
answers the guard, we already have people with those skills in
the hall. Finally Lug asks him if they have anyone who can per-

form *all* those tasks. The gatekeeper realizes they do not and admits Lug to the feast.

In medieval Wales, the supernatural shoemaker Lleu was related to the Gaulish Lugus and the Irish Lug. Life as a magical cobbler may seem like a definite step down for a god of arts, but in fact work with leather was a highly valued skill in earlier days. However the god Lugus may have evolved on his way to the medieval Welsh Lleu, the emphasis on his skill in crafts survived. And it's interesting to note that, in ancient Celtic times, an inscription from a group of shoemakers in Spain honored Lugus as their patron god.

Archaeologists have unearthed images of Lugus all over Gaul, confirming Caesar's statement of his importance and widespread worship. He is often associated with a goddess of wealth named Rosmerta, who seems to have been his consort. His name also shows up in ancient towns in Gaul and throughout the Celtic world—Lugudunum (the fort of Lugus) became Lyon in France and Leiden in Holland. Roman Lyon in fact held a festival to the god on August 1—the same date as the annual Lughnasadh festival for Irish Lug.

Caesar identifies the second Gaulish god, Apollo, as a healer of diseases, one of his chief roles in the classical world as well. We have a number of Gaulish inscriptions in which the name of Apollo is paired with that of a Celtic deity, Belenus (the shining one), though we also find him joined with other Gaulish gods. It was a common pattern in the ancient Mediterranean world to combine a Greek or Roman deity with the name of a native god or locality—much as we might distinguish Our Lady of Lourdes from Guadalupe or from Fatima. What we have in Gaul and beyond is in fact not one Celtic god but a whole array of Apollo-like gods, all with different attributes. Apollo Belenus was particularly popular in central Europe, northern Italy, and throughout Gaul, where he seems to have been identified with the sun. The fourth-century A.D. Roman writer Ausonius notes that even in late Roman times, Belenus had a temple near the English Channel. Apollo bears many other names as well, most significantly Borvo, the god of thermal springs. Hot springs in the ancient world, as in the modern, were noted for their healing powers—the very quality Caesar identifies with the Gaulish Apollo.

We might expect Caesar's third god, Mars, to have played a large role in war-loving Gaul, but references to him are vague. He is known by a bewildering number of names, such as Mars Albiorix (king of the world) and Mars Smertrius (the protector), many of which are single occurrences. It may be that Gaulish war gods were particular to each tribe and so not widespread enough to stand out in the archaeological or literary record. It could also be that the Romans discouraged Mars's cult after they took over Gaul—worshiping gods of arts or healing was fine, but war gods were too risky.

Jupiter, ruler of the sky, often bears the name Taranis on inscriptions; in the Gaulish language it means "thunderer." As a sky god comparable to the Greek Zeus and the Roman Jupiter, the Gaulish Taranis ruled over the heavens and made his will known through heavenly signs, especially lightning and thunder. But unlike his classical counterparts, Taranis was not the king of all the other gods. Lugus and the rest of the Gaulish pantheon did not quake before him as the Olympian gods did before Zeus. Still, Caesar ranks him among the leading divinities of Gaul, as is fitting in an agricultural society so dependent on the gentle rains of heaven.

The fifth and final of Caesar's chief Gaulish gods is Minerva, whom we met when the Celtic chief Catumandus worshiped her image at Massalia. She was a mother goddess known by many names throughout the Celtic world—Sulevia, Belisama, or Brigid among the later Irish. Minerva, like Lugus, was skilled in arts, though her talents were the practical concerns of the household attended to mostly by women. But she, like the Gaulish Apollo, was a god of healing and seems to have been closely tied with learning, poetry, and agriculture as well. This Gaulish goddess was a powerful deity who defies the neat categories we might wish to impose on her. In images, she is often joined with Lugus or other gods as a display of her great influence. Naturally enough, she appears to have been especially worshiped by women but also by anyone of the lower classes who felt a mother goddess was more approachable and perhaps more sympathetic. Her popularity and position in Celtic Gaul in fact bear a great resemblance to the role of the Virgin Mary throughout Christian history.

AFTER CAESAR describes the main gods of Gaul, he mentions a certain teaching of the Druids concerning Celtic origins: "The Gauls say that they are all descended from a single father, Dis— for this is the tradition handed down by the Druids. For this reason they count time by nights, not by days. In counting birthdays, months, and years, night always comes first." The Roman god Dis—also known as Pluto or Hades—was the ruler of the dim underworld, the land of the dead. As Dis was the Gaulish god of the dark netherworld, the Druids reckoned time beginning at nightfall rather than sunrise—just as Jewish tradition begins the day at sunset. Many ancient peoples believed that they were descended from a god—the Romans, for example, claimed they were descendants of Venus, while the Germans thought they were born of a god named Tuisto. Strange as it might seem to us that the Druids would pick a god of the dead for their origin stories, there are parallels in other mythologies, including that of early Ireland. The Irish Book of Invasions tells how Donn (the dark one) was drowned off the southwest coast of Ireland and buried on a small island called Tech Duinn, "the house of Donn" (modern Dursey Island off the coast of County Kerry). With his final breath he called for all his descendants to gather at his home after death. Elsewhere in early Irish literature, Donn's island is called the place where the dead join together. It may well be that these stories preserve a pre-Christian Irish myth in which the god Donn was their divine ancestor, to whose island they returned at death.

Whether or not the Gauls also believed they journeyed to a western island at death is hard to say, but there is a story from late antiquity that argues for this belief. The tale was handed down that on the coast of northern Gaul there once lived sailors who made their humble living fishing and trading—but they also took turns transporting the souls of the dead across the sea to Britain. On certain nights they would lie in their huts until the doors began to shake and a ghostly voice would call them forth. They were compelled by an inexplicable and irresistible urgency to go down to the shore, where strange and apparently empty vessels awaited them. Climbing into the boats, they took the oars in hand and pulled as if they were carrying a full load of passengers. The boats were sunk to the gunwales as the sailors rowed with miraculous speed westward to Britain, where the spirits of the dead would disembark to the cries of those who had come before.

IN THE FIRST century A.D., the Spanish-born poet Lucan recorded a few offhand lines about three Gaulish gods in his epic poem on the Roman civil wars of the previous century:

> Cruel Teutates satisfied by bloody sacrifice,
> Horrible Esus with his barbaric altars,
> And Taranis, more brutal than Scythian Diana.

Lucan, who was especially fond of using gladiatorial imagery in his writing, may not be the best source on Gaulish religion, but it's likely that whatever source he was drawing on had some contact with pre-Roman Gaul. It could even be that he makes use of some Posidonian passage that has been lost to us. But granting that Lucan is playing up the blood and gore aspect of Gaulish gods to titillate his Roman readers, he still provides us with the names of three Gaulish divinities, one of which we've met before. To make things even more interesting, ancient commentators on Lucan—presumably with their own sources—explain in gruesome detail the methods the Gauls used to sacrifice to each of these gods.

The name Teutates simply means "the god of the tribe" and could thus be attached to any number of gods throughout Gaul. His victims were reportedly killed by being plunged headfirst into a giant caldron and drowned. This is remarkably similar to a scene portrayed on the famous Gundestrup caldron from Denmark, though its Celtic origin has been questioned. On the caldron, a superhuman figure in striped pants and a very odd hat dunks a man into a vat, presumably as a sacrifice to himself. Lucan's second god, Esus, preferred his victims to be stabbed and then hung on trees—the same method used by ancient devotees of the Norse god Odin. The third god, Taranis, we have met as the Gaulish form of Jupiter or Zeus. Those unfortunate enough to be sacrificed to this god were, according to later commentators, placed in a large wooden cage and burned alive.

IN THE previous chapter, we saw the importance of the Gaulish god Ogmios (Hercules) to the Celts, even after the Roman conquest, but we also have brief bits of evidence on a large number of other divinities. Two of the most fascinating are a mother-son pair known as Matrona and Maponus. Matrona means "the divine mother," whose name is preserved in the Marne River in northeast France. There she was worshiped as the goddess of the river, according to one inscription. Because there are so many mother goddesses in ancient Gaul—including Caesar's Minerva—it's hard to know if the Matrona of the Marne was local or universal. Mother goddesses in fact usually appear on Gaulish inscriptions in groups of three, often holding wheat or flowers to represent their fertility function. In medieval Wales, Matrona is known as Modron, mother to Mabon— the Welsh form of the Gaulish Maponus, "the divine son."

Maponus appears as a cult figure in early Gaul and Britain, and is sometimes identified with Apollo. Maponus survives as the spirited young hunter Mabon in the Welsh tale *Culhwch and Olwen,* one of the earliest pieces of literature featuring King Arthur.

One god noted prominently in Gaulish inscriptions is Vulcan, the Roman god of blacksmiths. We don't know his Gaulish name, but his medieval Irish counterpart was Goibniu. As with shoemaking and crafts in general, the Celts placed a great value on the manufacturing arts, especially forging iron. The village smith knew the secrets of shaping essential household implements as well as weapons of war with his fire and hammer. The smith's prestige even grew to supernatural abilities, so that the previously mentioned *Breastplate* prayer attributed to St. Patrick asks for daily protection against blacksmiths as well as conjuring women and Druids.

The Gaulish god Cernunnos seems to have been particularly concerned with wild animals and may have been invoked before hunts. An early rock carving from Celtic Italy shows a horned god that may represent Cernunnos. A later carving from Paris certainly does, as it bears his name along with his curling antlers. Images of the Gaulish horned god often show him sitting cross-legged in a Buddha position unusual in Celtic art, sometimes surrounded by frolicking animals.

One final Gaulish god was so popular that she even made the transition to the Roman pantheon. Epona (the divine horse goddess) was adopted by the Roman cavalry and worshiped by horsemen throughout the empire. She appears in over two hundred Roman votive carvings from Britain to the Balkans, often sitting on a horse or on a throne between two steeds. In Welsh literature, the semidivine queen Rhiannon has many of her qualities and is particularly identified with horses. The mythical Irish equivalent, Macha, defeats all contenders on foot in a horse race, even though she is nine months pregnant.

There are dozens of other Gaulish gods and goddesses whose

names are recorded on faded inscriptions or in the pages of ancient manuscripts. Among the poorly known divinities are Nantosuelta, a water deity and perhaps household guardian; Damona, the cow goddess; Souconna, goddess of the Saône River; and Alisanus, god of rocks (or perhaps alder trees). By any measure, the ancient Gaul visited by Posidonius was a land of countless gods. Though we understand little of their worship, we know that their cults were immensely popular and continued long after the Roman conquest and the coming of Christianity.

FOURTEEN

DRUIDS

The cardinal teaching of the Druids is that the soul does not perish at death
but passes from one body to another.
JULIUS CAESAR, *GALLIC WAR*

THERE IS no area of ancient Celtic life that interested the Greeks and Romans more than the teachings and practices of the Druids. Posidonius carefully studied these Celtic priests and passes on important information concerning them in his surviving fragments. Other classical authors—Cicero, Tacitus, Pliny the Elder, and especially Julius Caesar—describe the Druids as well. But what do we really know about the Druids? It may surprise contemporary readers that all the Greek and Latin passages we possess on the ancient Druids would fit comfortably on a single page of paper. We actually know much more about early Celtic burial customs or medieval Irish beekeeping than we do about the celebrated beliefs of the Druids. But this isn't to say that our search for the Druids is in vain. Although we don't know everything we would like about the Druids, the scant information we do possess is both fascinating and surprising. For example, the Druids believed passionately in reincarnation, were highly organized, and included many women among their numbers. Misconceptions (ancient and modern) about the Druids are also common. They did not, in fact, worship trees or engage in frequent human sacrifice. There are certainly some aspects of Druidic behavior that will strike readers as cruel and barbaric, but we should see them in the context of the entire belief system of the Druids and realize that they lived in a world very different from our own.

Put aside for a moment everything you may have heard about the Druids—especially the gruesome stories of human sacrifice—and consider what Posidonius actually says about these men and women:

> There are three groups among the Gauls who are given special honor—bards, vates, and Druids. The bards are singers and poets, while the vates supervise sacrifices and study the ways of nature. The Druids also study nature but devote themselves to morality as well. The Gauls consider the Druids the most just of all their people, and so they are given the role of judge in all public and private disputes. In the past, they were even able to halt battles and bring an end to wars. Murder cases are especially given to the Druids for judgment. The Gauls believe that when condemned criminals are sacrificed, then the land will prosper. The Druids and other Gauls all say that the soul is immortal and the universe is indestructible, but that at some time in the future, both fire and water will prevail.

There is much to consider in this brief passage. First, the class of religious or semireligious officials in ancient Gaul was in fact made up of three separate groups—bards, vates, and Druids. Bards we have already met as highly skilled poets and powerful instruments of both glory and shame in Gaulish society. *Vates* (singular *vatis*) is in fact a term used by the Romans for their own prophets, but it was borrowed from the Celts of northern Italy. The vates performed sacrifices among the Gauls, but their role was much more important than simply acting as butchers. They assured that all sacrifices were done in accordance with sacred tradition; then, when the task was completed, they interpreted the results.

In another passage, Posidonius says of them: "They are a highly respected class of prophets. Through auguries and animal sacrifices they predict the future—and no one dares to laugh at them." Among the Greeks and Romans, the actual killing of a sacrificial animal could be performed by any number of people, including slaves. But among the Gauls it was the vates who carried out these crucial rituals from beginning to end. As their responsibilities included the proper interpretation of sacrifices and signs from heaven, they also had to be well-trained in the study of nature. Anyone needing to examine a sheep's liver or flashes of lightning for messages from the gods had better know a great deal about animal physiology as well as meteorology.

Posidonius says the Druids were also keen students of nature, but their application of this knowledge was on a much broader scale. This study of natural phenomena was important, but Posidonius states that an even more important role of the Druids was to act as dispensers of justice. All public and private—or as we would say, criminal and civil—cases were brought to the Druids for settlement. The Gauls clearly believed the Druids were a class set apart and genuinely admired their special devotion to justice and honorable behavior. They could even step between warring armies and force hostile tribes to lay down their arms. Given the hot-blooded nature of Gaulish warriors, that was indeed a sign of respect.

Posidonius also notes that the Druids sacrificed condemned criminals, but consider the context of the statement. Yes, the Gauls without a doubt performed gruesome human sacrifices that were overseen by the Druids, but such rituals were unusual. Posidonius states that "the Gauls will keep a criminal under guard for five years, then impale him on a pole in honor of their gods. They will then burn his body on an enormous pyre along with first fruits of the land." Doubtless the poor, suffering criminal gathered little comfort from the fact, but this particular rite of human sacrifice seems to have occurred only once every five years as part of a harvest festival. It was not a daily slaughter for some bloodthirsty god but an exceptional effort at restoring balance to nature for the good of the tribe. Of course, Posidonius says elsewhere that war prisoners could be used for such sacrifices, but this may have been only when criminals were not available.

The civilized people of the Mediterranean could shake their heads in fascinated horror at the reports of Gaulish human sacrifice, but they had plenty of skeletons in their own closets. Homer speaks of human sacrifice in the *Iliad*, and the archaeological record suggests it was at least occasionally practiced in the Greek Bronze Age. The Phoenicians, master explorers that they were, regularly sacrificed children to their gods. Even the Romans practiced human sacrifice in extraordinary circumstances until the third century B.C. In a Greek and Roman world where infanticide was practiced on an enormous scale, where women and children were regularly slaughtered in war, and where the Romans saw death in the gladiatorial games as entertainment, the occasional practice of human sacrifice among the Celts was a relatively minor event.

The actual act of human sacrifice, though rare in Gaul, was certainly gruesome. Posidonius explains that such rituals could involve a bizarre form of divination. This description includes such detail that we have to wonder if Posidonius witnessed it himself:

The Gauls have an especially strange and unbelievable method of predicting the future for the most important affairs. They first anoint a human victim, then stab him with a small knife in the chest just above the diaphragm. They watch the man carefully and interpret future events by the way he falls, how his limbs shake, and the way that his blood spurts on the ground.

As horrifying as this sacrifice must have been to observe, Posidonius does note that it was used by the Druids only in the most crucial circumstances.

THERE IS archaeological evidence to support the claims of Celtic human sacrifice. We've already seen the recent discoveries of ritually slain headless bodies from far to the east in Galatia, but there are similar finds on the other end of the Celtic world. In 1984 peat cutters near Cheshire, England, came across the body of a man in his twenties who had been killed and placed facedown in a bog named Lindow Moss. The police were called, and investigations were begun in nearby towns to identify any recently missing persons—but it turned out Lindow Man (as he was later named) had been dead for almost two thousand years. Tests determined that he had died sometime in the first century A.D., in a most unusual way. First he was struck on the head, but only hard enough to stun him into unconsciousness. Then he was strangled, with the cord tied in back, and finally his throat was cut. It's unlikely that Lindow Man was simply the victim of some ancient British hooligans; the complex manner of his death suggests a ritual act. Also intriguing is the fact that stomach analysis reveals his last meal consisted partially of mistletoe, a plant connected with the Druids by the Roman author Pliny. Visitors to the British Museum in London can now file past the well-preserved remains of Lindow Man and see for themselves a probable victim of Celtic human sacrifice. But Lindow Man is not alone. A number of similar bodies have been discovered in northern and western Europe. None matches exactly the manner of death described by Posidonius, but it's likely there were as many variations of human sacrifice as there were Celtic tribes.

WHAT IS far more interesting about the ancient Druids than their occasional use of human sacrifice is what Posidonius says about their teachings. According to him, the Druids taught that the human soul was immortal and indestructible. Posidonius expands on this belief: "The Gauls follow the doctrine of Pythagoras. They teach that the human soul is deathless and after a certain number of years passes into another body to begin a new life. Because of this belief, some people will throw letters on funeral pyres so that the dead might read them."

In the ancient world, belief in the immortality of the soul was not universal, nor was the afterlife normally viewed as a happy condition. Most ancient people believed that the good and bad alike lived after death, but only in a dark, dreary netherworld without joy. The Greek hero Achilles, encountered by Odysseus on his journey to Hades, says that he would rather be a live slave to the poorest farmer in Greece than rule over the kingdom of the dead. But there were exceptions to this belief, such as the doctrine of reincarnation advocated by the sixth-century B.C. Greek philosopher and mathematician Pythagoras. The ideas of Pythagoras sound very much like the cycle of death and rebirth found in Hinduism and Buddhism—in fact, it is possible that he was influenced by Eastern beliefs. Thus it's natural that when Posidonius or any other classical writers refer to Celtic beliefs in reincarnation, they speak in terms of familiar Pythagorean teachings, even though the Druids would never have heard of Pythagoras.

One fascinating aspect of this Celtic teaching is that the rebirth of the soul was not immediate. Many years could pass between a person's death and his next incarnation. In the meantime, the soul apparently existed in a spiritual world that could be reached through the portal opened by a funeral fire. The scene is a touching one that must have been witnessed by Posidonius many times. At the end of a funeral, those Gauls who had lost loved ones—children, spouses, parents, friends— walked forward one by one to place their letters on the burning pyre in the hope that their messages would reach the other-world.

The statement of Posidonius that the Druids also believed the universe to be indestructible, but that one day it would be overcome by fire and water, is as baffling as it is mesmerizing. What could this possibly mean? Posidonius has clearly recorded a teaching he heard from the Druids in Gaul, but we have it only in the briefest form. It's likely that the Greek philosopher is here reporting a prophetic story of the end of the world— what Christian theology calls eschatology. This short sentence is the only hint we have in all of ancient Celtic religion about such a teaching. Early Christians and some Jews also believed in an apocalyptic end to the world, followed by a new heaven and earth. Ancient Norse mythology speaks of Ragnarok—a grim day when the gods themselves would be destroyed, though hope of a new beginning remained. The Druids apparently had similar stories in which, though the universe was ultimately indestructible, the world in which we live would be overcome by both flood and fire. It's possible and even likely that they told of a new world coming into being after this destruction, but we will never know for certain.

THE SECOND great source of information on the ancient Druids is Julius Caesar. During his seven-year conquest of Gaul, Caesar had plenty of opportunities to become familiar with Gaulish culture and religion. He had certainly read Posidonius and clearly borrows from him on several occasions, but Caesar fills in many details about the Druids that are missing in our surviving fragments of Posidonius, such as their organization and training. Caesar makes little distinction between bards, vates, and Druids, grouping them all together in a single class of respected professionals. The training of all three groups must have overlapped in many ways, with specialization coming only at the latter stages of education. Thus, when Caesar speaks of the Druids, he may be including bards and vates as well.

According to Caesar, the Druids formed a priesthood with a strong organization and well-defined hierarchy that spread across tribal boundaries: "Among the Druids there is one supreme leader who holds authority over all the rest. When this chief Druid dies, he is succeeded by whoever is most qualified. If there are several contenders for the position, the Druids all take a vote—though they have been known to contend for the title with armed force."

Gaulish tribes were fiercely independent and could rarely cooperate on anything, even under outside threat. Thus, to have a united priesthood with a chief Druid that spanned the whole land was both remarkable and highly useful. The Druids were in a position to act as arbiters in disputes between tribes—even in the midst of battle, as we have seen. There must have been considerable tension at times between Gaulish rulers and the Druids, but any king would have realized how helpful it was to have an organization that could cross borders unmolested and settle conflicts in negotiation with other Druids. For the Druids, the kings and warriors in turn imposed order on the contentious tribes so that their priesthood could operate and prosper. As in medieval Europe, with its ambitious rulers and international Church, the parties of power may not have always liked one another, but they definitely needed one another.

As with modern organizations, Caesar notes that the Druids enjoyed getting together for an annual convention: "At a certain time every year, the Druids all gather together at a sacred spot in the land of the Carnutes tribe—a place thought to be the center of all Gaul. People with disputes come from everywhere to have the Druids decide their cases." If these meetings were anything like those of current professional associations, they involved as much socializing as business. They must have provided an opportunity for Druids of various tribes to meet old friends, make new connections, and discuss common problems. But there were also serious judicial matters to decide, just as there were at the similar gathering in Galatia at the meeting place called the Drunemeton. The Carnutes, in whose lands the annual meeting was held, occupied the area to the southwest of Paris, around the town of Chartres. In fact, there's a case to be made that Chartres Cathedral, a soaring monument of medieval architecture, was built on the very site of the Gaulish Druids' holy gathering. Early Christians often took over the sacred places of earlier pagan religions as a way of easing the transition to their faith by using locations long considered holy.

Caesar also mentions human sacrifice overseen by the Druids, but he again emphasizes that it was the exception rather than the rule. He also describes what is certainly the most colorful form of Gaulish human sacrifice: "Some Druids will build enormous figures with arms and legs made out of twigs and fill them with living persons. They then set these structures on fire and burn all the victims alive." The famous Gaulish wicker man filled with dozens of writhing victims would challenge the structural skills of any modern engineer, but the Gauls apparently did burn sacrificial victims alive from time to time. It was a popular and grisly form of execution for many cultures, from the ancient Gauls to the fires of the Inquisition. Caesar adds that in the past, the Druids would burn faithful slaves and servants alive on the funeral pyres of their masters.

CAESAR NOTES that Druids were not restricted to Gaul. In fact, he asserts that Britain was considered the heartland of the Druidic tradition: "It is said that the Druids began in Britain and from there came to Gaul. Even today, those in Gaul who wish to study their traditions most diligently travel to Britain." Whether or not the Druids in fact arose in Britain or were always present in Celtic society is hard to say. If the Druids were a relatively late movement in the Celtic world, that might explain why there is no mention of the order until Posidonius. Perhaps the Druids began as an organized priesthood only in the last few centuries B.C. This would explain why the Celts of

Spain, who migrated to the Iberian Peninsula early, never mention the Druids. In any case, it's interesting that in medieval Irish stories, Britain is also a place for higher education in the religious arts. The Irish prophetess Fedelm, for example, is returning from study in Britain when she meets the warrior queen Medb in the epic *Táin Bó Cuailnge.*

Caesar emphasizes repeatedly the unique place of the Druids in Gaulish society. The Druids were even exempted from that most onerous duty in any century—paying taxes. But unlike the warrior class, it seems that Druids were made, not born. Caesar says many young people were drawn to the study of Druidic tradition by the numerous advantages such a life offered and willingly committed themselves to the necessary training. Others, perhaps not as willing, were strongly encouraged to become Druids by their parents. Whether they were enthusiastic volunteers or pushed by mothers and fathers, the failure rate for would-be Druids must have been extremely high given the intense and lengthy education needed—up to twenty years according to Caesar.

The reason for such extensive training is that everything the Druids had to learn to practice their art needed to be memorized in verse form: "It is said that in the schools of the Druids, students must learn many verses. . . . They are not allowed to write down any of these sacred teachings, even though they record all manner of other public and private business in Greek letters." Archaeologists have found a number of such records in the Gaulish language but using the Greek alphabet. Why weren't the teachings of the Druids ever written down? Caesar offers two reasons that make perfect sense. First, the fact that Druidic teachings were purely oral and passed only from master to students kept them secret from everyone else in Gaulish society. This not only created a sense of mystery around the Druids' knowledge but had the very practical effect of making the Druids indispensable for all matters of religion, law, science, and history. If there was, for example, a legal dispute over a king's inheritance or questions on the best way to worship a particular god, a Druid—and only a Druid—could be called forth to recite the appropriate precedent in verse from a vast mental storehouse.

Caesar also says that the Druids learned all their teachings in poetic form as a way to improve the faculty of memory. Just as the Greeks memorized Homer's *Iliad* and *Odyssey* or Roman schoolboys learned their ancient laws by rote, Gaulish Druids learned their entire tradition—everything from theology and natural history to medicine and genealogy—by memory. The fact that all this information was in verse is crucial. As a mental experiment, try to remember the best lecture or sermon you ever heard. You may recall vague images, scattered words, or even entire lines of a gripping speech, but the whole is forever lost. Now search your memory for all the old songs residing there. Most people can recall dozens or even hundreds of lyrics once they hear the first few words. Likewise, the Druids memorized all of their teachings in verse as an aid to memory. All a Druid had to do in any situation to remember the proper words for a ceremony or the solution to a thorny problem was recall the right verses learned during years of training.

Like Posidonius, Caesar states that this education included much more than performing the proper religious rituals. The central teaching of the Druids was the immortality of the soul and the doctrine of reincarnation. Caesar takes the very practical attitude that this belief was useful for encouraging bravery on the battlefield—if death is merely temporary, then soldiers will not be afraid to die. But reincarnation was only the beginning of a young Druid's education: "They have many other teachings as well that they pass on to their students—the motion of the stars, the size of the earth and the whole universe, the ordering of nature, and the power of the immortal gods." Oh, that we had all these Druidic teachings still! But the fiercely oral nature of the Druids' wisdom, which kept it exclusively a part of their religious order, also meant that it perished without being written down. All that remain are a few bits and pieces preserved in classical authors, along with a very limited tradition in later Celtic stories.

CAESAR wasn't the only Roman leader to have firsthand experience with Druids in the decades after Posidonius. In a dialogue with his brother Quintus, the orator and consul Cicero speaks of a meeting he held with an important Druid: "I know there are Druids in Gaul because I met one myself—Divitiacus of the Aedui tribe—a former guest of yours who praised you highly. This man claimed to know a great deal about the workings of nature based on what the Greeks call *physiologia*—the search for causes and phenomena. He also predicted the future using augury and other methods."

Divitiacus was a remarkable character who also appears in Caesar's writings, though the Roman general never mentions that he was a Druid. The Aedui were a powerful tribe of central Gaul that Posidonius probably visited himself. In the 60s B.C., just before Caesar's invasion, they were led jointly by Divitiacus (who was pro-Roman) and his brother Dumnorix (anti-Roman). Divitiacus had come to Rome to plead for help against invading Germanic tribes. During this visit, he met with Cicero and many other Roman leaders. Cicero had long been interested in divination, so it was natural that he would jump at the chance to talk with an articulate and knowledgeable Druid from distant Gaul. Divitiacus even demonstrated a few Gaulish divination techniques for the curious Roman.

Divitiacus undoubtedly played up his skills as best he could for Cicero in an attempt to win his support for the Gaulish cause, but there's little reason to doubt this firsthand report. Like Posidonius and Caesar, Cicero describes the Druidic study of nature but uses a Greek term—*physiologia*—that had been a favorite of intellectuals since Aristotle. It was in fact a word that Posidonius himself was fond of using, especially to explain the differences between various approaches to science. Someone

who observes and describes natural phenomena, according to
Posidonius, does a necessary and important task. But the one
who practices *physiologia* goes beyond measurement and description to delve into the crucial question of *why* things happen.
Just as Posidonius had both observed and theorized on the nature of tides in Spain, the Druids both studied natural phenomena and attempted to explain the reasons why the universe
behaves the way it does. It's no wonder Posidonius was so interested in a group that shared his combined practical and theoretical approach to the natural world.

AFTER THE relatively benign views of Posidonius, Caesar, and
Cicero in the first century B.C., there is a noticeable shift in
classical attitudes toward the Druids. A possible explanation for
this change is the Roman invasion of Britain under the emperor Claudius. The classical world had known about Britain
since at least the time of the explorer Pytheas in the fourth
century B.C., but few people gave the island any thought. Caesar staged two brief military campaigns in southern Britain in
55 and 54 B.C., but these were never designed to be anything
more than quick, punitive raids. In the years after Caesar, however, the Romans became increasingly interested in Britain and
its resources. Several rulers, including Caligula, considered
adding the island to the empire, but Claudius decided the time
was right in A.D. 43.

One probable justification for the invasion of Britain was the
destruction of the last stronghold of the supposedly horrible
Druids. After all, Caesar himself had said that Britain was the
epicenter of the Druidic world. Patriotic and order-loving Romans could scarcely bear such a barbaric cult just across the
channel from their Gaulish territory. If it turned out later that
the Druids weren't really a threat to Roman civilization—well,
there were still plenty of taxes and slaves to be gained from a
conquered Britain.

The most vivid description of the British Druids is given by

the historian Tacitus. He recounts the Roman attack on the
Welsh island of Anglesey in A.D. 60, a key part of the decades-
long war on the tribes of Britain:

> The densely packed armies of the Britons were on the oppo-
> site shore. All around them ran wild-haired women waving
> sticks looking like the Furies themselves. The Druids were
> everywhere praying to their gods and calling down curses.
> These sights terrified our soldiers, who had never seen any-
> thing like them before. The legions stood there exposed to the
> enemy's weapons as if their limbs were paralyzed. But soon
> they pulled themselves together and listened to their com-
> mander, who was yelling at them not to be scared of a mob of
> crazy women. Finally the troops pressed forward, slaughter-
> ing everyone in their way. We left behind a garrison there that
> destroyed the sacred groves dedicated to their wicked super-
> stitions. The Druids, after all, consider it their religious duty
> to cover their altars with human blood and practice divina-
> tion by studying human entrails.

Behind the lurid propaganda that Tacitus dishes out for his
Roman audience, there are some interesting facts. During
World War II, construction of an airfield on Anglesey uncovered
a site called Llyn Cerrig Bach, where over a hundred valuable
objects had been ritually deposited in a shallow lake in the first
century A.D. Offerings to Celtic gods were commonly placed in
water throughout Europe, but the finds on Anglesey were particularly rich—swords, caldrons, shields, chariot pieces, slave
chains. It's possible this was an offering of desperation made by
the Druids as they watched the Roman armies drawing near.
The description Tacitus gives of the frenzied women on Anglesey is also revealing. His scene may be filled with deliberate
melodrama, but it is one of several classical accounts that feature female Druids.

o o o

AFTER TACITUS, Roman authors speak of the Druids mostly in the past tense, often as a historical curiosity. Before he was killed investigating the eruption of Vesuvius in A.D. 79, the Roman writer Pliny rejoiced that the legions had recently wiped out the murderous cult of the Druids, but—like many Romans—he retained a fascination with their religious practices. In his encyclopedic *Natural History,* Pliny in fact provides us with our most detailed accounts of actual Druidic rituals.

The first rite of the Druids begins with the collection of mistletoe. Pliny writes that the Druids considered this parasitic plant sacred—especially if it grew on oak trees—and called it "all-healing." The Druids would search far and wide for an oak tree, then cut its mistletoe only at night on the sixth day of the waxing moon, when the moon's power was still increasing but not yet halfway through its course. (Pliny adds that the Druids measured time strictly by the movement of the moon.) The act of cutting the mistletoe was elaborate: "First they held a sacred meal under the oak tree, then led forward two white bulls whose horns had never before been bound. A Druid dressed in white then climbed the tree and cut the mistletoe with a golden sickle, letting the sacred plant fall onto a white cloak." After this, the bulls were sacrificed and the mistletoe was brewed into a drink that would restore fertility to livestock and act as a remedy for poison.

The second Druidic ritual described by Pliny also involves the collection of a sacred plant, but in an even more precise manner. The Druids plucked an herb they called *selago* without any iron instrument by passing their right hands through openings on their left sleeves, as if they were stealing it. The harvester—who had to be barefoot—wore the usual white clothing, having first made an offering of bread and wine to the gods. This plant was supposedly good as a charm against evil, while the smoke from burning it was effective against eye diseases. A similarly gathered plant called *samolus* was placed only in watering troughs as it was good for bovine disorders, but the one plucking it was not allowed to look backward.

The third and most incredible Druidic ritual described by
Pliny centered on the quest for a magical serpent stone. According to Pliny, the Druids would search out a mass of snakes that
had curled themselves into a ball. The snakes in this writhing
group would produce a hard, egglike object called an *anguinum*
from their secretions, which they would then toss into the air. A
watchful Druid had to be ready to catch this ball in a cloak before it hit the ground. But that was not the end. The angry
snakes would then invariably chase the Druid until their pursuit was cut off by a stream or river. A proper serpent stone
could supposedly float upstream, even if it were covered in gold.
Pliny claims to have seen a serpent stone for himself, saying it
looked like an apple covered with octopus suckers. These stones
were probably fossilized tree resin or some kind of exotic
seashell, but Pliny says that the Druids believed they were wonderful good-luck amulets.

THE YEARS PASSED in Roman Britain and Gaul, but the
Druids did not altogether disappear. In A.D. 235, the Roman
emperor Alexander Severus was driving the latest invasion of
Germanic tribes out of Gaul when he met a most unusual
woman—a Druidess who warned him not to place too much
faith in arms alone. Just a few decades later, a young soldier and
future emperor named Diocletian was staying at a tavern in
Gaul reportedly run by a Druidess. One day when he went to
settle his bill, his hostess told him he was a cheapskate: "Diocletian laughed and said, 'I'll be more generous when I'm the
emperor.' 'Don't laugh,' the Druidess shot back. 'You will be
emperor after you kill the boar.'"

Years later Diocletian did become emperor, after killing an
assassin named Aper (Latin for "boar"). In the 270s, the emperor Aurelian regularly consulted a Druidess to determine the
future, especially whether or not his family would continue to
hold the throne. These three female Druids may be a far cry

from the respected priests and prophets of earlier Gaul, but they
still maintained the prophetic functions described by Posidonius and Caesar.

FOR THOSE DRUIDS who didn't open taverns, there were
other occupations readily available. The Romans never wanted
to wipe out peaceful and orderly native religions, so the many
temples of Gaul that continued to offer simple animal sacrifices
to Gaulish and Roman gods were encouraged by the authorities.
These temples all needed priests—what better candidates could
there have been than Druids and their descendants? The
Roman poet Ausonius, in the late fourth century A.D., writes of
one such Druidic family in northern Gaul:

> You are descended from the Druids of Bayeux,
> If the stories are true,
> And you trace your lineage and fame
> From the temple of Belenus.

According to Ausonius, other Druids became teachers and professors. Thus, the Druids never really disappeared from Gaul.
With the taint of human sacrifice long behind them, their religious training and education were welcomed by the Romans.

THE STORY of the Druids, however, does not end in Roman
Gaul and Britain. Across the sea in Ireland, the Druids continued to prosper for centuries. Medieval Irish stories must always
be used with care in a search for historical fact, but the many
references to the Druids and their role in Irish mythology argue
for their power on the island—a power that faded gradually
with the coming of St. Patrick and Christianity. Irish legend
frequently speaks of Druids as counselors of kings, respected
prophets, and supervisors of important religious rituals.

A more solid historical source for Druids in Ireland is early

Irish law. These ancient texts tell the sad story of the Druids' decline as Christianity spread through the land. The Irish *drui* or Druid was still a respected and feared figure, even in the sixth century A.D. Noble children were instructed by Druids, and oaths were sworn before them. But over the next two hundred years, those Druids who did not convert to the new faith were reduced to a low status, earning a meager living making charms and potions.

FIFTEEN

CONQUEST

They were a brave enemy—through the whole battle lasting from noon to
sunset, no Roman ever saw the back of a Gaulish warrior.
JULIUS CAESAR, *GALLIC WAR*

WITH HIS RESEARCH on the Gauls completed, Posidonius
left behind the Celtic world of Druids, bards, and screaming
warriors to return to the civilized lands of the Mediterranean.
He must have carried many rolls of papyrus notes on the Gauls
and their peculiar customs as he made his way south down the
Rhone River into Roman territory. Returning to Massalia, he
once again settled in a villa to rest from his journey, sort
through his materials, and enjoy the pleasures of dining without
severed heads gazing down upon him. From Massalia he sailed
home across the Mediterranean Sea to Rhodes, where he was to
spend the remaining forty years of his life.

We know only bits and pieces of what happened to Posidonius
during the years between his return from Gaul and his death in
the mid–first century B.C. He settled down in Rhodes to write
and teach, with his school eventually becoming the center of
Stoic studies for the Greek and Roman world. But we know that
Posidonius was not just an ivory tower philosopher—he was
deeply involved in local government and served as a *prytanis,* or
city magistrate, for Rhodes. In 87 B.C., just a few years after his
return from Gaul, the citizens of Rhodes sent him on a diplomatic mission to Rome. He was likely chosen both for his political skills and because of the contacts he had made with Roman
leaders during his previous visit. This was a particularly dan-

gerous time for anyone to visit Rome. The Italian allies had just staged a massive rebellion that had been crushed by the legions. The Roman general Sulla had then launched a coup against the state, followed by the capture of Rome by Marius and his forces in 87. The subsequent terror in the streets was unusually bloody, even by Roman standards. Citizens deemed unfriendly to the current cause were condemned without trial and decorated the Forum with their heads. Into this melee walked Posidonius—who must have compared the behavior of the Romans with that of the Gauls and wondered which ones were truly the barbarians.

After returning to Rhodes, Posidonius began a writing career that rivaled Aristotle's in range and output. He wrote well-respected books on philosophy, astronomy, physics, geology, ethics, zoology, mathematics, and many other subjects. But his *History* was the major work of an immensely productive life. It was composed of fifty-two books exploring every aspects of life and culture from around the Mediterranean. In it, he recorded the observations he had gathered during his travels in Gaul.

Greeks and Romans all flocked to Rhodes to hear Posidonius lecture and to study with the most famous philosopher of the day. In the early 70s B.C., young Cicero was a student of Posidonius and bragged that they became great friends. Later Cicero invited Posidonius to write a work celebrating his own consulship—an offer Posidonius graciously declined. In the 60s, the Roman general Pompey stopped by to hear a lecture during his campaign to rid the Mediterranean of pirates. After conquering the eastern Mediterranean a few years later, Pompey again arrived in Rhodes to visit Posidonius but was told the philosopher was suffering from a severe case of gout. Still, Pompey ordered his military standards to be lowered before the door of Posidonius's home out of respect.

Pompey—along with Marius, Sulla, and especially Julius Caesar—was one of the major figures in the transformation of Rome from a republic to an empire. The old rules, designed for governing a small city, were no longer effective in ruling the vast lands Rome had gathered under its wings. By the middle of the first century B.C., Pompey and Caesar, along with Marcus Crassus, formed a three-man junta called the First Triumvirate to rule over Rome. Caesar was definitely the junior partner in this coalition, but he managed to secure for himself the governorship of Illyricum (roughly the former Yugoslavia) across the Adriatic, along with northern Italy (Cisalpine Gaul) and the Roman Province of southern Gaul (Transalpine Gaul). Caesar was a canny politician as well as a brilliant general, so his choice of a base in Cisalpine Gaul was no mere chance. From the Po valley he could keep a close eye on affairs in nearby Rome, as well as use the territory as a launching point for military conquests. Caesar, like any ambitious Roman, desperately needed money—and the amounts he required could come only through conquest of rich, new territories. At first it was probably his goal to move east into the Dacian kingdom on the lower Danube, but events in Transalpine Gaul soon diverted his attention to the west.

Caesar, being fluent in Greek, had certainly read the *History* of Posidonius. It's possible he had even met the philosopher during a previous visit to Rhodes. In any event, he was quite familiar with the vast resources and potential of Gaul. He knew Roman businessmen were making a fortune trading with the tribes of central Gaul beyond the Roman-controlled coast. He also was well aware of the problems the Gaulish tribes were having with the Germans across the Rhine.

Germanic tribes such as the Suebi, under their chief Ariovistus, were regularly raiding Gaulish lands. But the Gauls, displaying the eternal weakness of the ancient Celts, refused to cooperate to drive out their common enemies. The Sequani Gauls in the east even beseeched the Germans to help them recover lands that they had previously lost to the neighboring Aedui. This was just the opportunity the wily Ariovistus had been waiting for. The Suebi were all too happy to drive the

Aedui from Sequani lands, but when the war was over, Ariovistus refused to leave. He began systematically to settle his own Germans on Gaulish lands previously belonging to the Aedui. These longtime friends of Rome sent ambassadors, including the Druid Divitiacus, to the Senate to plead their case, but Ariovistus had arrived first with gold to bribe the Roman nobility to look the other way.

The Gaulish Helvetii tribe of western Switzerland had watched all these events with growing alarm and decided it was time to cut their losses and run. They had long been on the front lines against the Germans, and with the growing strength and influence of the Ariovistus, their future did not look promising. The Helvetii leaders initiated a plan for their tribe to migrate westward across Gaul to the relatively peaceful lands along the southern Atlantic coast. The Aedui, being along this path of migration, once again appealed to Rome for help. But this time Caesar was in place as a governor just itching for fortune and glory. He sent word to the Helvetii to stay put in Switzerland, but they ignored his warnings. Thus, in the spring of 58 B.C., Caesar marched north with his legions to the Helvetii lands around Lake Geneva. The conquest of Gaul had begun.

CAESAR and his Roman army met the defiant Helvetii in a pitched battle near the Aedui town of Bibracte—a region probably visited earlier by Posidonius. Caesar drew up his forces on a hill and sent away all the horses, even his own, so that no Roman would be tempted to flee. The Gauls charged, but the Romans launched a volley of spears that stuck in the Celtic shields. Many Gauls were so frustrated by shields covered with Roman spears that they threw them away and fought without protection. The Romans forced the Helvetii down the hill until the Gaulish cavalry swung around and attacked the Romans from the rear. This encouraged the Helvetii to redouble their efforts, and the Gauls pounded at the Roman army from two directions, much as the Cisalpine Gauls at Telamon had faced a double-sided attack by the Romans two centuries earlier. But after a long and fierce battle, Roman discipline overcame the bravery of Gaulish warriors. Although many Helvetii survived the fight and fled, it was an awesome display of Roman power over the Gauls in the heart of their own land.

Instead of seeing the danger posed by such Roman success against their own countrymen, the Gaulish kings flocked to Caesar and petitioned him to push Ariovistus and his Germans out of Gaul. This put Caesar in the ideal position of protector and spokesman for the Gauls. He then made a very modest request of Ariovistus to stop settling Germans on Gaulish soil, but the chieftain brashly replied that his Germans would instead conquer Gaul all the way to the Atlantic Ocean. This was like waving a red flag in front of a bull to Caesar, who unleashed his army and routed the Germans, destroying the power of Ariovistus and removing the German threat from Gaul for many years.

At this point, the Gaulish kings probably thought Caesar would go home to Italy and leave them to run their tribes as before. Their first hint that the old days were over began when Caesar set up a winter camp for his army in the territory of the Aedui, far from the Roman Province along the Mediterranean coast. With this move, Caesar made it clear that the Romans were in Gaul to stay.

THE FIRST Gaulish tribes to react to Roman annexation were not, as one might expect, the Aedui or the tribes of central Gaul but the Belgae, on the northern frontier near the English Channel. In 57 B.C., Caesar rode north and defeated the Belgae after fierce resistance, then dispatched part of his army westward past Normandy and conquered the Gaulish tribes in this area, even though they had done nothing to provoke such action. The next year, he defeated the maritime tribe of the Veneti in Brittany and sent his forces south along the coast all the way to Spain. To any attentive observer among the Gauls, Caesar's intentions were perfectly clear—he was encircling central Gaul as a prelude to final conquest.

The year 55 B.C. dawned in Gaul with Caesar in firm control of all the land except the densely populated and rich center of the country. Caesar may have hoped that these more civilized tribes would capitulate voluntarily and thus spare him the trouble and expense of devastating their lands. He would have been quite happy to leave the profitable lands of the Arverni, Carnutes, and other wealthy tribes untouched, except for the introduction of Roman officials to tax the Gauls and recruit their sons into his army. Caesar gave them time to consider the future while he launched a quick punitive raid against Britain. Some British tribes had allegedly aided the Gauls in their fight against Rome, but it's likely that Caesar was more interested in the glory of first landing Roman troops on this island at the edge of their world.

Late in the summer of 55 B.C., Caesar gathered together his aides and Gaulish allies to learn everything he could about Britain in preparation for his crossing. This raid was clearly meant as a brief reconnaissance in the hope of future expeditions: "Caesar thought it would be a good idea at least to land on the island, learn something about the nature of the Britons, and scout out the countryside, harbors, and landing places." The Gauls were not very helpful in providing information about Britain, since few had been there and those who had made the journey had merely landed on the southern coast.

Caesar then made one of the few foolish moves of his military career by staging a hasty and poorly planned assault on the Britons near the white cliffs of Dover. He loaded his army into landing craft and crossed the channel, but the ships were too big for the shallow waters of the British coast. The Roman troops were stopped far out from the shore and forced to leap with full armor into heavy, pounding seas up to their chests. The Britons meanwhile launched volleys of spears at the Roman troops while they struggled toward shore, all the time attacking the Romans from horseback.

After losing many men, Caesar finally gained the upper hand and drove the natives back from the shore. He marched only a little way inland, to the area south of London, before turning back. But Caesar was successful in learning much about the British tribes during this raid and during a more lengthy expedition the following year. Like Posidonius, he was very impressed with the skilled chariot warfare of the Celts. He also noted that the southern British tribes were similar to the Gauls and quite civilized. He records that they used coinage and imported many goods from abroad. Among their more peculiar customs, he notes, was their aversion to eating rabbits and their habit of painting their faces blue for battle. He also claimed that British men lived in groups of about a dozen and had wives in common.

GAUL HAD BEEN quiet during Caesar's excursions into Britain, but in the winter of 54 B.C., all of Caesar's carefully laid plans for a peaceful transition of Gaul to Roman rule began to unravel. One Belgic chieftain, named Ambiorix, managed to lure an entire legion out of its winter quarters near the Ardennes Forest and destroy it. This success emboldened all of Gaul to revolt against the Romans.

The Nervii tribe of northern Gaul managed to besiege and almost destroy a second Roman army commanded by Cicero's brother Quintus, but Caesar made a lightning march from his camp north of Paris to relieve him. This brief success was soon overshadowed by the most threatening force yet to face Caesar in Gaul—the Gaulish chieftain Vercingetorix. This nobleman of the Arverni tribe in south-central Gaul was unlike anyone Caesar had encountered among the fiercely independent and uncooperative Gauls. Vercingetorix was the son of a man who had been put to death because he sought too much power within his tribe. Like his father, Vercingetorix (whose name appropriately means "leader of warriors") aspired to great heights. He tried to raise an army against Caesar but was thrown out of his hometown by his uncle and the other leading citizens, who didn't want trouble from the Romans. Vercingetorix then borrowed a trick from the Roman founders Romulus and Remus by gathering together all the outcasts and disaffected young men of the region to form his own private army. In time, the young Arvernian leader convinced his tribesmen to follow him on his great crusade for Gaulish liberty. He then did something very unusual for a Celtic leader. Instead of marching his small army against Caesar into certain but glorious slaughter, he patiently recruited troops from all of Gaul to his banner. The Celts had finally realized that the only way they could drive Caesar and his Romans out was to act as a single nation under one ruler.

Vercingetorix was as meticulous as a Roman quartermaster in laying in supplies and telling each tribe exactly what it had to contribute to the cause. To those Gaulish warriors under his command who refused to be governed by orders, he meted out harsh punishments. Minor cases of rebellion were dealt with by cutting off a man's ear and sending him home in shame. Serious offenders were burned to death before the whole army. By careful planning and strict discipline, Vercingetorix created a powerful army of Gauls that could stand up to and defeat the Romans.

Finally, Vercingetorix and his army were ready. In a daring move worthy of Caesar himself, the Gaulish leader decided to take the fight to Roman territory. He sent his army south into the Roman Province in an attempt to draw Caesar away from his troubled legions in northern Gaul. With Caesar absent, the hope was that the isolated Roman legions would be destroyed by the Belgae and northern tribes. The Gauls almost reached the Mediterranean coast before Caesar drove them back. Caesar checked the Gaulish movement south, then made an unexpected dash with his army across snow-covered mountains to attack the Arvernian homeland. He then rapidly marched north to relieve his troubled armies.

But Vercingetorix was just getting started. Over the next few months, he forced Caesar to engage in a series of exhausting sieges of Gaulish towns while avoiding open battle. Caesar was not used to a Gaulish leader who could control his spirited warriors and hold back from a fight. At the fortress of Gergovia in Arvernian lands, Caesar's impatient troops themselves acted against orders and came close to being defeated by the Gauls. After this Roman debacle, the myth of Caesar's invincibility was destroyed, and almost every Gaulish tribe, even the normally pro-Roman Aedui, joined the rebellion of Vercingetorix.

Vercingetorix called the Gauls together and explained that the only way to drive the Romans from their land once and for all was to sacrifice individual desires to the greater glory of the Gaulish nation. The Roman armies had to be deprived of food, and the only way to do this was to burn every Gaulish farm that they might use for resupply. Avoid direct confrontation with Caesar, he urged, and instead pick off his army bit by bit as they search for grain among the burned-out fields of Gaul: "If this seems harsh or cruel to you men of Gaul, then consider— how much worse is it than having your wives and children dragged off by the Romans into slavery and slaughter? For that is the fate of the conquered."

This scorched-earth policy of guerrilla warfare was effective against the Romans until Vercingetorix made the mistake of withdrawing his forces to behind the walls of the fortress town of Alesia. Whether he was seeking a brief rest for his army or hoped to tie down Caesar in a protracted siege, once he was within the walls of this formidable citadel, Caesar had him trapped.

Like Celtiberian Numantia, the site of Alesia was perfect for resisting vast armies. A high, broad hill between two steep river valleys prevented direct assaults. Vercingetorix thought he could safely watch as Caesar's troops wore themselves out besieging the town. In addition, Gaulish forces outside the citadel could attack Caesar's undefended troops from behind and slowly force the Romans into withdrawal or surrender. What Vercingetorix had not counted on was the skill of Roman engineers and the unconventional thinking of Caesar. Instead of placing his army around the town in camps, Caesar began construction of an enormous earthen wall, eleven miles in length, that encircled the town. The Gauls inside Alesia awoke one morning to see themselves trapped within a huge and well-defended ring of Roman forces. Even more surprising, the siege wall faced not merely inward toward the town but outward as well. Secure inside the double walls of his circular fort, Caesar could both contain Vercingetorix within Alesia and hold off any Gaulish forces sent to relieve him.

In spite of these formidable defenses, Vercingetorix sent messengers to the Gaulish tribes asking for troops to attack the Romans and relieve his army of eighty thousand men within the walls of Alesia. He then gathered together all the food and cattle in the town and calculated that his forces could endure the siege for at least a month. When the messengers dispatched from Alesia arrived at their destinations, the tribal rulers gathered together in a council. They rejected the pleas of Vercingetorix to send every available man against the Romans, claiming that it would be too difficult to feed and control such a crowd of warriors. Instead they sent a smaller force, gathered from all the tribes of Gaul except the Bellovaci, just north of the Seine River. These stubborn holdouts had not learned cooperation even at this late stage of the war and asserted that they would face the Romans at their own time without interference from other tribes (they were later crushed by Caesar).

The Gaulish relief force marched boldly to Alesia, confident that no army on earth could withstand it. Meanwhile, inside Alesia, matters were growing desperate. More than a month had gone by without any word from the outside. Supplies were gone and the army was starving, along with the civilian population. Vercingetorix and his troops had no idea that help was on the way, so they called a council to consider their options. Some of the leaders urged surrender, others advocated an immediate at-

tack on the Romans while they still had their strength. Then
one Gaulish chieftain, named Critognatus, stepped forward and
spoke:

> I won't waste my words arguing with those who want to sur-
> render us to slavery. They have no place as Gauls, let alone as
> members of this council. I instead want to address those who
> urge an attack, for in such daring there is a memory of the
> warriors we used to be! But I say to you, it is a weakness not
> to wait for the proper moment.

Critognatus then urged the council to consider a most audacious plan. Eat those inhabitants of Alesia who were too old or
injured to fight—for the alternative was slavery or death for all.
Desperate as they were, Vercingetorix and the council could not
bring themselves to such a drastic action. Instead they forced all
the remaining civilian population out of the town to reduce the
number of mouths to feed. The poor inhabitants of Alesia—
thousands of old men, women, and children—approached the
Roman siege walls weeping and begged to be allowed out of the
city, even if it meant being sold into slavery. Caesar, however, refused and sent them back to Alesia to starve.

Finally the army of Gauls arrived to relieve the siege. Caesar knew what was coming and positioned his forces along his
inside and outside walls, all around their circumference, then
ordered his cavalry out to harass the Gaulish relief force. The
Gauls looked down in amazement at the double-sided defenses
of the Romans but were still eager to launch an attack. They
sent their own cavalry, along with a few archers and spearmen,
against the Roman horsemen. The Romans were driven back
by this mixed force and withdrew within their walls. A great
cheer broke forth from the Gauls both outside and inside Alesia. Surely this was the end of the Romans in Gaul—they
would soon be squeezed between two irresistible forces. The
Druids accompanying the army may already have been plan-

ning what sort of golden bowl they would make out of Caesar's skull.   ♦

Vercingetorix and his troops poured out of Alesia against the Roman inner walls while tens of thousands of Gaulish warriors swarmed toward the outer walls of the camp. Every Gaul strove to impress his fellows by acts of bravery, just as each Roman sought the eye of Caesar as they fiercely resisted. The battle raged on from noon till sunset, with neither side able to gain the upper hand. Finally, German horsemen in the Roman army managed to surround the Gaulish cavalry and destroy them, giving the Romans just the chance they needed to force the Gaulish infantry back to their camp. The Gauls who had come out from Alesia returned to the town, bruised but not beaten.

That night the Gauls secretly busied themselves making equipment to scale the Roman camp walls. Early in the morning, while it was still dark, thousands of Gaulish warriors armed with ladders and grappling hooks silently made their way to a weak spot in the Roman defenses. On signal, they shouted to their countrymen inside the walls of Alesia to launch every spear and stone they had down at the Romans. The town troops responded, and Vercingetorix then moved his forces out to attack the Romans. In darkness, both Romans and Gauls ended up injuring as many of their own forces as of their enemy. Vercingetorix rushed to fill in the Romans' trenches and scale their inner walls but discovered that the relief force had already withdrawn because they feared a Roman attack with increasing daylight. Facing the Romans alone, he returned to Alesia yet again.

After two defeats, Vercingetorix knew he needed a daring plan. Some local soldiers told him that there was a spot on the northern side of the Roman walls that Caesar had not been able to enclose completely because of the lay of the ground. Vercingetorix sent a cohort of troops to this vulnerable place in the Roman lines and ordered them to wait for his signal. He then led his forces from the city and launched an all-out attack. Both sides knew this was the final battle. The Gauls realized they had to break through the Roman lines this day or their fate was sealed. The Romans knew that if they could hold back the Gauls, the end of the war would be near.

Caesar watched the battle unfolding, sending extra troops here and there to patch up any weaknesses. Suddenly word came that a force of concealed Gauls had attacked a weak spot on the northern perimeter and was on the verge of swamping the Roman defenders. After sending every spare troop he possessed, Caesar was finally able to fend off the Gaulish attack and repel Vercingetorix and his army back to Alesia. Many thousands of Gauls in the relief force were slaughtered by Caesar's troops as they fled the field. Some were taken prisoner and sold into slavery, but others managed to escape the Romans and return to their home tribes.

The next day Vercingetorix gathered together the survivors from his forces for one final council inside Alesia. I fought only for Gaulish liberty, he declared, and never for my own glory. He then offered himself as a prisoner to the Romans, dead or alive, as they wished. When the Gaulish messengers arrived at the Roman camp, Caesar ordered that all the weapons and every warrior be brought forth to him. On the bloody field beneath Alesia, he set up a pavilion to receive the Gaulish surrender. Thousands of warriors marched forth from the town with whatever dignity they could muster and threw down their weapons at Caesar's feet. Each was handed over to a Roman soldier as a war prize, to be quickly converted into cash by waiting slave dealers. As they marched off in chains, they knew the dream of Gaulish freedom was over, as was their own cherished liberty. Finally, Vercingetorix rode forth and presented himself to Caesar. The Roman general had no plans to let the Gaulish leader escape with simple slavery or a quick death. Vercingetorix was bound and taken to Rome for public display and humiliation. Six years later, after Caesar had crossed the Rubicon and conquered all rivals in his bid for rule of Rome, Vercingetorix was led on a parade of triumph through the Roman Forum and finally executed.

Gaulish resistance continued for another year, especially among the Belgae in the north, but the days of independent Celtic rule on the European continent were over. The Galatians, Celtiberians, Italian Gauls, and now finally the Celts of Gaul had one by one fallen to Rome. By the year 51 B.C., the world of the Celts described by Posidonius was gone. It is perhaps a cruel coincidence that this same year probably saw the death of Posidonius on his island home of Rhodes. One can imagine the final days of Posidonius and wonder if he heard the news of Caesar's conquest before he passed away. The brave barbarians the philosopher had visited, dined with, and described to the world were now just another nation among the vast crowd of Roman subjects. There would be no more single combat between Gaulish warriors, no kings, and no Druids—at least not as in the old days. The Celts would be absorbed into the wider Greco-Roman world, but they were not gone forever. Across the sea in Britain and Ireland—and even in Gaul itself—Celtic life would continue for many centuries to come.

THE CELTIC
HERITAGE

*I often heard Agricola say that he could conquer Ireland with just one
Roman legion and a few auxiliary troops. It would certainly be a useful lesson for the British if they were surrounded by Roman troops on all sides and
freedom was banished from sight.*

TACITUS, *AGRICOLA*

AFTER THE SURRENDER of Vercingetorix, Gaul slowly settled into life as part of the Roman world. It was Roman policy
to change as little as possible in newly conquered territories.
The Gaulish tribal hill forts often became Roman towns and
centers of local administration. Gaulish nobles who were
deemed loyal to Rome were encouraged to become part of the
local government. Beginning with the emperor Claudius, the
Celtic nobility was even allowed to serve in the Roman Senate,
though few achieved this lofty role in practice. Children of
wealthy Gaulish kings, warriors, and Druids were taught Latin
and given a classical education equal to that found in any city
of the empire. The nobility kept the lands it had controlled before the conquest and still dominated the free peasant farmers,
who noticed little change with the shift from Gaulish to Roman
control. For young Gaulish men with high spirits and a longing
for glory, the Roman army was always looking for a few good
men. Gaulish recruits were prized for bravery and their ability
to learn quickly. After a period of service in the legions, the

Gauls returned home to their tribes with a good knowledge of soldiers' Latin and often a grant of the coveted Roman citizenship.

Although human sacrifice ended with the conquests, the religion taught by the Druids flourished in Gaul for centuries. Celtic sanctuaries continued to be used and often incorporated Roman deities into their worship. The Gauls still prayed to Lugus, Epona, and all the other gods of the Celtic pantheon—and in their own language. The Romans never tried to impose Latin on any of their conquered lands. If the inhabitants wanted to speak their native tongue—be it Aramaic, Punic, Greek, or Gaulish—the Romans couldn't care less, as long as they paid their taxes on time. Roman judges were even known to hear cases presented in Gaulish through interpreters. The Gaulish language continued to be spoken throughout Gaul for at least five hundred years after Caesar. The second-century Christian bishop Irenaeus of Lyon complained in one letter that his Greek and Latin were becoming horribly rusty because he had to translate everything into Gaulish for his parishioners. Many of the writings we have in the Gaulish language actually date from after the Roman conquest, such as the magical tablet from the religious cult of women at Larzac described in Chapter 10. But Gaulish inscriptions could be playful and even bawdy. A set of clay spindle whorls from eastern France bear flirtatious graffiti written by young men and women working in the textile industry of Roman Gaul. Like those of young people of many lands and times, their thoughts seemed to focus mostly on drinking and sex. Some of the graffiti is in Latin, some in Gaulish, but much is in mixture of the two. One young man tried to gain the attention of a girl working nearby with flattery:

Hello, good-bye—you're beautiful!

Other would-be Romeos tried a more direct approach:

Give in, city girl.

Dear girl, are you willing?

Some hoped that liquor would smooth the way:

Pretty girl, drink some wine.

Hey, beautiful, give me a beer.

One young man even tried a lewd pun:

Come on, girl, take my kiss!

The Gaulish word *bussuton,* translated "kiss" in this case, can also mean "penis"—which definition the young man had in mind I leave to the reader's imagination. One young woman's response to such pleas shows that Gaulish women had lost none of their self-confidence:

I'm a girl who is good and beautiful.

After the defeat of Vercingetorix by Caesar, the only independent Celtic kingdoms remaining in the ancient world were found in Britain and Ireland. The two brief Roman raids on Britain in 55 and 54 B.C. were followed by almost a century of neglect by Rome. Only in A.D. 43 did the Romans move on the island, beginning three decades of progressive conquest punctuated by a few revolts, such as that of the Druids of Anglesey and Queen Boudicca in A.D. 60. Soon after Boudicca was defeated, the Britons faced the Roman general Agricola. As described by his son-in-law Tacitus, Agricola swiftly moved past York to the borders of Scotland. After crushing the northern British tribes around Edinburgh, he swept eastward to the final and greatest battle, at Mons Graupius on the North Sea. In the year 84, Celtic warriors for the final time faced the Roman legions in a decisive conflict. The Celts fought with great bravery, as they always had, but the outcome was an inevitable repeat of Telamon, Numantia, and Alesia.

The Romans withdrew from Scotland and eventually built Hadrian's Wall as a northern limit to their empire. To the north, the native British and Pictish tribes continued a life largely untouched by the Romans. To the south, Britain was divided into administrative units governed by Roman appointees. As in Gaul, life for most of the Celts was little changed, aside from the payment of taxes to Rome and recruitment into the army for those young men seeking wider frontiers. Noble families pressed their sons to learn Latin as a means of advancement in society, and beautiful villas were built across southern Britain by these Romanized Celts.

IN SPITE OF General Agricola's plans to conquer Ireland, the island remained beyond the reach of the Roman Empire. Pytheas of Massalia had sailed past Ireland in the fourth century B.C., and traders had certainly visited since early times, but the first historical descriptions of Ireland are nothing but slanderous rumors. Strabo, who preserved many of Posidonius's descriptions of Gaul, claimed that Ireland was a bitterly cold island inhabited by incestuous, gluttonous cannibals. Other writers described a milder climate where cattle could explode from overeating the abundant grass, but all the earliest writers agreed that the Irish themselves were the worst sort of barbarians. Still, by the late first century A.D., Tacitus said that Ireland was being visited by Roman merchants—a fact borne out by archaeological discoveries. The second-century Greek geographer Ptolemy described Ireland's coastline in detail, noting landmarks such as the Boyne River in the east of the island and the Shannon River in the west. The Irish traded gold and slaves to the Romans, as well as huge wolfhounds destined for the entertainment of the crowds of Rome.

Ireland was divided into over a hundred quarreling and fiercely independent kingdoms, much like pre-Roman Gaul on a smaller scale. Druids and poets still exerted a powerful influence in a land almost untouched by Christianity. But over the next two centuries, as the new religion spread, the Druids lost their power while that of the poets grew. The old pagan stories were written down by bards and even clergy eager to record their native traditions. These myths and legends blended with classical traditions imported from abroad to create one of the earliest bodies of literature from the Middle Ages.

The most extensive tradition from medieval Ireland is the famous *Táin Bó Cuailnge*—a grand series of tales built around a great cattle raid by Queen Medb and her Connacht warriors against the Ulstermen and their champion, Cú Chulainn. Homer took the Greek tales of Troy and wove them into a seamless narrative of incredible depth and style, but the *Táin* is something different. In it we find a collection of myths and sagas that never felt the unifying hand of a master poet. Reading these tales, we sit before the hearth of an Irish king and hear the voices of many storytellers, all creating a world long past. The similarities to the Gaulish world described by Posidonius are amazing—Druids, feasting, heroic warriors, fearless women, greedy kings—but all are seen through the eyes and imaginations of the medieval Irish audience. Just as Homer fused the world of Bronze Age Greece with elements of his own era centuries later, the *Táin* combines the lost age of pre-Christian Ireland with the culture of the Irish Middle Ages.

IN THE END, the heroic Celtic society described by Posidonius survives only in memory. But in the last century, it was still possible to find pockets of Celtic culture maintaining at least some of the old ways. On the storm-tossed Blasket Islands, off the southwest coast of Ireland, the rare visitor in the early twentieth century would have met a leader still known as a *rí* or king. On these rocks sticking out of the Atlantic, the islanders spoke Irish until they were finally evacuated to the mainland in the 1950s. A number of the Blasket Islanders wrote of their lives and the final years of the island. One was Tomás O'Crohan, whose memoir *The Islandman* has become a minor classic of Irish literature. In it he tells of a life of struggle and frequent death but also joy and freedom on the edge of the world. In one story, he relates how the resident bard of the island interrupted him as he was collecting turf to heat his cottage and proceeded to tell him a long-winded tale from memory. The author was anxious to go about his business, but he didn't dare invoke the wrath of a Celtic poet: "I didn't care much for what he had to say, but I was rather shy of refusing to sit down with him. Besides, I knew that if the poet had anything against me, he would make a satire on me that would be very unpleasant." Thus, even in the twentieth century, the Blasket Islands maintained the ancient Celtic tradition of storytelling and satire as Posidonius first described it.

TIME LINE

B.C.

c. 1200 Troy and Mycenaean Greek kingdoms fall

c. 700 Hallstatt period of Celtic history begins in central Europe

Homer's *Iliad* and *Odyssey* composed

c. 600 Greek colony of Massalia founded on the Mediterranean coast of Gaul

490 Greeks defeat Persians at Battle of Marathon

c. 450 La Tène era of Celtic history begins

420s Herodotus first mentions the Celts in his *History*

399 Socrates executed in Athens

390 Gauls sack Rome

334 Alexander the Great invades the Persian Empire

320s Pytheas of Massalia sails to northern lands of Europe

279–78 Gauls attack Delphi; Galatians cross into Asia Minor

225 Romans crush Gauls of Italy at Telamon

c. 135 Posidonius born

90s (?) Journey of Posidonius to the West

58–51 Julius Caesar conquers Gaul

c. 51 Posidonius dies

A.D.

43 Romans begin conquest of Britain

60 Revolt of Celtic queen Boudicca

A GLOSSARY OF
GAULISH WORDS

In the last few decades, scholars and archaeologists have begun to uncover the ancient Celtic language of the Gauls. Here are just a few of the more interesting words that Posidonius may have heard on his travels. A complete collection can be found in Xavier Delamarre's *Dictionnaire de la langue gauloise* (2003).

anandogna	stranger, foreigner
anatia	soul
antumnos	world of the dead
argos	hero
atir	father
bardos	poet
bena	woman
braca	pants
brixta	magic
bussuton	kiss (or "penis")
carros	chariot
cattos	cat
caxtos	slave
ceruesia	beer
cladios	sword
cu	dog
deuos	god
druides	Druids
epos	horse
genos	family
gnata	girl
maruos	death
matir	mother

nemeton	sanctuary, sacred place
orcos	pig
rigana	queen
rix	king
sindiu	today
teuta	tribe
uatis	prophet
uimpos	beautiful
uindos	white
uiros	man

oinos, allos, treis one, two, three

PRONUNCIATION GUIDE

Celtic languages have a reputation for being difficult to pro-
nounce. Sometimes—as with modern Irish and Welsh—this reputation is well-deserved, but Celtic languages of classical times
were much simpler. The following is a short guide to the more
common elements of Celtic pronunciation.

GAULISH

The ancient Celtic language of Gaulish that Posidonius heard
on his travels was very similar to Latin and Greek in both
structure and pronunciation. As in Latin, almost all the consonants and vowels are read as they appear on the page. *C*'s are always hard (*k*, not *s* or *ch*), as are *g*'s (as in *go*, never *j*). As in
classical Latin, a *v* would be pronounced as a *w*. For example:

droungos	drun-gos
trimarcisia	tri-mark-is-i-a
Veleda	we-le-da

WELSH

Welsh is the modern Celtic language most closely related to
Gaulish, but its spelling and pronunciation have undergone radical changes in two thousand years. Any language that can
produce town names like *Llanfairpwllgwyngyllgogerychwyrndrob-
wllllandysiliogogogoch* (St. Mary's Church in the hollow of white
hazel near a rapid whirlpool and St. Tysilio's red cave) is going
to be a challenge for nonnative speakers. In short, *w* and *y* can
be consonants or vowels, *ch* sounds like the final sound of German *ich*, and *ll* (represented here by *L*) is found in few other
languages of the world, apart from the dialect of the Inuit of

Greenland—try pronouncing it by making a regular *l* sound
without vibrating your throat.

Culhwch	kil-huch
Lleu	Lai
Llyn	Lin
Pwyll	pwiL

OLD IRISH

Old Irish, like Welsh, evolved rapidly from its early Celtic roots.
Long vowels are marked by an accent (e.g., *cú*), and *ch* is pronounced in the back of the throat, as in Welsh. Consonants
standing between vowels are usually softened, so that, for example, *t* becomes *d* and *d* becomes the sound of the final consonant
in English *bathe* (shown below as *dh*).

Ailill	a-lil
Cathbad	kath-badh
Cú Chulainn	koo chulan
Medb	medh-av
Samain	sa-wan
Táin Bó Cuailnge	tan bow kual-nya

NOTES AND
SUGGESTED READINGS

There are many good books available on the ancient Celts. Here are those I have found most helpful, arranged according to chapter topics.

All the translations in the book are my own, but for the sake of clarity in certain passages I have occasionally paraphrased the ancient texts. I therefore include references to the Greek, Latin, and Celtic sources for anyone who would like to read the originals. Most of the selections used in this book, along with many others, can be found in my *War, Women, and Druids* (2002), an anthology in translation of the most important classical sources on the ancient Celts.

INTRODUCTION
Epigraph: J. R. R. Tolkien, "English and Welsh," in *Angles and Britons* (1963, 29). In the same article (41), Tolkien notes his debt to a modern Celtic language in the *Lord of the Rings* trilogy: "The names of the persons and places in this story were mainly composed on patterns deliberately modelled on those of Welsh (closely similar but not identical)."

Passages: Ptolemy's record of the meeting between Alexander the Great and the Celts is recorded in Strabo, *Geography* (7.3.8) and Arrian (*Anabasis* 1.4). The boastful response of the Celts to Alexander is strikingly similar to that of the Irish warriors to the Ulster king Conchobor in the medieval *Táin Bó Cuailnge* (trans. Kinsella 1969, 247).

1. POSIDONIUS
Epigraph: Suda, Testimonia 1a (Edelstein and Kidd T1).

Passages: Posidonius's fragment on the Apameans at war is recorded by Athenaeus, *Deipnosophistae* (4.176—Edelstein and Kidd F54); Herodotus on the Egyptians is from his *History* (2.35), as is the passage on the cloven-footed inhabitants of northern Asia (4.25–26); Polybius discusses his own methods of research in several sections of his lengthy *History* (3.59, et cetera); Posidonius's view of God is found in the *Placita* of Aetius (1.7.19—Edelstein and Kidd F101); Epictetus's austere advice is from his *Handbook* (1, 3).

Readings: Modern scholarship on Posidonius has been advanced immeasurably by the four-volume annotated edition of his testimonia and fragments edited by L. Edelstein (vol. 1) and I. G. Kidd (vols. 1–4). Also valuable are J. J. Tierney's article "The Celtic Ethnography of

Posidonius" in *Proceedings of the Royal Irish Academy* (vol. 60, sec. C, no. 5, 189–275) and Daphne Nash's "Reconstructing Poseidonios' Celtic Ethnography: Some Considerations" in *Britannia* 7 (1976, 111–126). Thomas Cahill does an admirable job of surveying ancient Greek civilization in his *Sailing the Wine-Dark Sea* (2003), while *Greece and the Hellenistic World* (eds. J. Boardman, J. Griffin, and O. Murray, 1992) is a favorite of students (or at least professors). No one beats Peter Green for elucidating Hellenistic history, especially in his *Alexander to Actium: The Historical Evolution of the Hellenistic Age* (1990)—his sections on Hellenistic philosophy are especially helpful. For those with a taste for adventure, I recommend Michael Wood's *In the Footsteps of Alexander the Great* (1997), along with the accompanying PBS series video of the same name. The History of Herodotus (available in many good English translations) is a wonderful introduction to Greek ethnography, so enjoyable that C. S. Lewis recommended it for lunchtime reading. *The Edges of the Earth in Ancient Thought* (1994) by James Romm is a great modern survey of the subject. There are many excellent surveys of Greek philosophy, though my favorite look at the philosophers before Socrates is *Early Greek Philosophy* (2002) by Jonathan Barnes. Plato, in spite of his lofty reputation, is one of the most readable and entertaining ancient thinkers. Start with his *Apology*—in which Socrates takes on the Athenian establishment—and work up to the *Republic*, where you'll find one of the earliest manifestos of gender equality and other radical ideas. Aristotle is a little tougher, but his *Nicomachean Ethics* is full of great practical advice and profound truths. You can read the whole *Enchiridion* (handbook) of the Stoic Epictetus over your morning coffee, while the longer *Meditations* of the Roman emperor Marcus Aurelius presents many of the same ideas.

2. BEGINNINGS

Epigraph: Ephorus, *On Europe* (via Strabo, *Geography* 1.2.28).

Passages: Herodotus twice mentions the Celts in his *History* (2.33 and 4.49).

Readings: The best general introduction to the early Celts is Barry Cunliffe's *The Ancient Celts* (1997), which I have used frequently throughout this book. For almost all the chapters that follow, I refer the interested reader to the appropriate sections of this excellent book. The *Atlas of the Celtic World* (2001) by John Haywood is a great visual reference for early Celtic culture and expansion. Ruth and Vincent Megaw's *Celtic Art* (1990) is the best work available on the artistic culture of the ancient Celts. I also recommend *The Celts* (ed. V. Kruta, 1997) and H. D. Rankin's *Celts and the Classical World* (1987).

3. DELPHI

Epigraph: Callimachus, *Hymn* 4.171–175.

Passages: The inventory list bearing the inscription "Celtic iron weapons" is from *Inscriptiones Graecae* ii² 1438, lines 7–8; Aristotle's comments are found in his *Nicomachean Ethics* (3.7.6–7); Ephorus is quoted in Strabo, *Geography* (4.4.6); Sopater's aside on Celtic human sacrifice is from Athenaeus (15.160e); the banquet trap of Theopompus is found in Athenaeus, *Deipnosophistae* (10.443); Pausanias, *Description of Greece* (10.19.5–23.14) is our major source for the Celtic invasion of Delphi and the one I primarily use in this chapter, but also see Justin, *Epitome* (24.6–8); the first Pausanias passage is 10.19.12; the quotation on Celtic butchery at Callium is from Pausanias (10.22.2–4), while the Delphic oracle to Croesus is from Herodotus, *History* (1.53).

Readings: Most of the early sources on the Celts are included in *The Celtic Heroic Age* (2003) by John Koch and John Carey. Particularly good studies of Celtic archaeology and culture of this period can be found in *The Celtic World* (ed. Miranda Green, 1995).

4. GALATIA

Epigraph: St. Paul, Epistle to the Galatians (3:1).

Passages: Anyte's poem is from the *Greek Anthology* (7.492); Strabo's description of Galatian tribes and political organization is found in his *Geography* (12.5.1); the Galatian word *droungos* comes from the fourth-century bishop Epiphanius, *Against Heresies* (2.239), in the context of a strange group of Galatian Christians who placed their fingers on their noses during worship; the inscription from A.D. 166 is from Stephen Mitchell's *Regional Epigraphic Catalogues of Asia Minor II: The Inscriptions of North Galatia* (no. 75); the passage on Galatian mercenaries is from Justin's *Epitome* (25.2), while the gravestones of Galatian soldiers near Alexandria are from B. Cook's *Inscribed Hadra Vases in the Metropolitan Museum of Art* (no. 17) and A. Merriam, "Painted Sepulchral Stelai from Alexandria," *American Journal of Archaeology* 3:261–68 (no. 3); the Galatian graffiti from Egyptian Thebes is found in W. Dittenberger's *Orientis Graeci Inscriptiones Selectae* (no. 757); Polybius (21.38) tells the story of Chiomara via Plutarch's *Virtuous Deeds of Women* (22), which also records the tale of Camma (20).

Readings: An absolutely essential source for the study of ancient Galatia is Stephen Mitchell's two-volume *Anatolia: Land, Men, and Gods in Asia Minor* (1995). Those who wish to sift through the fragments of Celtic speech in Asia Minor might try my own *Galatian Language* (2001). The evidence for human sacrifice in ancient Galatia is vividly presented in *Archaeology*, vol. 55, no. 1 (January–February 2001, 44–49).

5. ROME

Epigraph: Polybius, *History* (2.29).

Passages: Posidonius's view of Roman dining habits is found in Athenaeus, *Deipnosophistae* 6.275 (Edelstein and Kidd F267); Joseph Eska discusses Lepontic inscriptions in his article "Continental Celtic" in *The Cambridge Encyclopedia of the World's Ancient Languages* (2004, 857–880); Livy's account of the Gaulish invasion of Italy and sack of Rome is from his history of Rome (5.33–49); Polybius describes the Battle of Telamon in his *History* (2.25–31); Wolfgang Meid covers the Gaulish-Latin inscription from northern Italy in his *Gaulish Inscriptions* (1992, 20–22).

Readings: Anyone interested in the Celts in Italy should start by reading the pertinent sections of Livy and Polybius, but two modern introductions to the subject are J. H. C. Williams, *Beyond the Rubicon* (2001), and Peter Ellis, *Celt and Roman* (1998).

6. SPAIN

Epigraph: Silius Italicus, *Punica* (3.340–343).

Passages: Posidonius and his measurement of the earth are from Cleomedes, *De motu circulari corporum caelestium* (1.10.50–52— Edelstein and Kidd F202); the philosopher's sojourn in Cádiz and elsewhere in Spain is best discussed by Strabo in his *Geography* (3.2.9—Edelstein and Kidd F239, 3.3.4—F224, 3.4.15—F243, 3.5.7–9—F217–18, and 13.1.67—F237); Herodotus tells the story of the first Greek in Spain in his *History* (4.152); the *Ora Maritima* passage is from the fourth-century A.D. poem by Rufus Festus Avienus (108–119); the description of Celtiberian soldiers is from the Latin poet Lucilius, quoted by Nonius in his *De compendiosia doctrina* (227.33); the most accessible English texts of Celtiberian writing are in Wolfgang Meid's *Celtiberian Inscriptions* (1994), with the two from this chapter 32 and 46–47.

Readings: One of the best discussions of the Celtiberians is by Majolie Lenerz-de Wilde, "The Celts in Spain," in *The Celtic World*, edited by Miranda Green (1995, 533–551). For the general topic of trade among early Atlantic cultures, I highly recommend Barry Cunliffe's *Facing the Ocean* (2001). The subject of Celtic inscriptions in Spain is more difficult for the nonspecialist reader to access, but—aside from Meid's book mentioned previously—the essay "Continental Celtic" by Joseph Eska and D. Ellis Evans in *The Celtic Languages*, edited by Martin Ball (1993, 26–63), is a great start.

7. MASSALIA

Epigraph: Justin, *Epitome of the Philippic History of Pompeius Trogus* (43.3).

Passages: Posidonius records his observation on apes in North Africa via Strabo, *Geography* (17.3.4—Edelstein and Kidd F245), where life in Liguria is also found (3.4.17—Edelstein and Kidd F269 and 5.2.1—F268); the stories of Massalia's foundation and early years are recorded in Athenaeus, *Deipnosophistae* (13.576), and Justin, *Epitome* (43.3, 5); the surviving fragments of Pytheas's voyage are collected in Christina Horst Roseman's *Pytheas of Massalia: On the Ocean* (1994); the name Uxisame is quoted by Strabo (1.4.5), who also notes Posidonius's comment on the Tin Islands (3.2.9—Edelstein and Kidd F239).

Readings: A. Trevor Hodge does a great job tracing the history of Massalia and other Greek colonies in Gaul in his *Ancient Greek France* (1998). The explorations of Pytheas are superbly recounted in Barry Cunliffe's *The Extraordinary Voyage of Pytheas the Greek* (2002).

8. TRIBES AND KINGS

Epigraph: Posidonius, *History,* book 23, as found in Athenaeus, *Deipnosophistae* (4.152—Edelstein and Kidd F67).

Passages: The Irish *Audacht Morainn* (*The Testament of Morann*) comes from the edition of Fergus Kelley (1976, passages 12–13, 21).

Readings: Gaulish kingship and the structure of society are discussed and illustrated in Simon James, *Exploring the World of the Celts* (1993), as are Celtic agricultural practices and village life. Fergus Kelly details medieval Irish kingship in *A Guide to Early Irish Law* (2003, 17–26).

9. WARRIORS AND HEAD-HUNTING

Epigraph: Posidonius, *History*, via Diodorus Siculus, *History* (5.29).

Passages: The descriptions of chariot warfare, nakedness in war, single combat, and head-hunting among the Gauls are also taken from Posidonius via Diodorus Siculus (5.29–30); Posidonius's discussions of Gaulish clothing, weapons, and trumpets are from Diodorus Siculus (5.30); the single combat of Titus Manlius and the Gaulish warrior is from Livy (7.9–10); Strabo quotes Posidonius on head-hunting in his *Geography* (4.4.5—Edelstein and Kidd F274).

Readings: A short but reliable source on Gaulish warriors is *Celtic Warrior: 300 B.C.–A.D. 100* (2001), written by Stephen Allen and wonderfully illustrated by Wayne Reynolds. The recent discoveries of Gaulish temples in northern France are presented in "Gallic Blood Rites" by Jean-Louis Brunaux, the excavator of Ribemont, in *Archaeology* vol. 54, no. 2 (March–April 2001, 54–57). I must respectfully disagree with Professor Kidd's assertion (Kidd 2.2, 937) that Posidonius could have gathered all the evidence he needed for Gaulish head-hunting near Massalia. The Roquepertuse temple was in fact destroyed by fire almost a century before the philosopher arrived in Gaul, and the Romans had put a stop to such practices elsewhere when they conquered southern Gaul in the second century B.C. (Strabo, *Geography* 4.4.5—Edelstein and Kidd F274).

10. WOMEN

Epigraph: Posidonius, *History,* via Diodorus Siculus, *History* (5.32). *Passages:* The remarkable story of Onomaris is from the anonymous *Tractatus de Mulieribus Claris in Bello;* her story is discussed by D. Ellis Evans in "Onomaris: Name of Story and History?" from *Ildánach Ildírech* (1999, 27–37); medieval Irish laws regarding women are found in Fergus Kelly's *Guide to Early Irish Law* (2001, 68–81); the jewelry of Celtic women is described by Diodorus Siculus (5.27), and homosexuality by the same author (5.32); the aversion of Gaulish men to being seen with their young sons is from Caesar's *Gallic War* (6.18–19), as is his description of Gaulish dowries and the power of husbands over their wives; Posidonius's island of women is from Strabo (4.4.6—Edelstein and Kidd F276), while Pomponius Mela's is from the *De chorographia* (3.6); discussion of the lead tablet from Larzac may be found in Wolfgang Meid's *Gaulish Inscriptions* (1992, 40–47); Ammianus Marcellinus mentions Gaulish women warriors in his *History* (15.12); the story of Boudicca is from Tacitus, *Agricola* (16) and *Annals* (14.31–37), along with Dio Cassius, *Roman History* (62.1–12). *Reading:* An excellent study of Boudicca is found in Graham Webster's *Boudica: The British Revolt Against Rome* A.D. *60* (1993).

11. FEASTING

Epigraph: Athenaeus, *Deipnosophistae* (4.154). *Passages:* An English translation of *The Story of Mac Dá Thó's Pig* may be found in *Early Irish Myths and Sagas* by Jeffrey Ganz (1981, 179–187), while the original Old Irish is presented in *Scéla Mucce Meic Dathó* (ed. Rudolf Thurneysen, 1986); Phylarchus's story of Ariamnes is from Athenaeus, *Deipnosophistae* (4.150); Athenaeus quotes all the included passages of Posidonius in the *Deipnosophistae* (4.151–52—Edelstein and Kidd F67 and 4.154—F68); Diodorus Siculus passes on the observations of Posidonius in his *History* (5.28); *Bricriu's Feast* is also found in Ganz's collection (219–255).

12. BARDS

Epigraph: Posidonius, *History,* book 23, as quoted in Athenaeus, *Deipnosophistae* (6.246—Edelstein and Kidd F69). *Passages:* The story of Luvernius comes from book 23 of Posidonius's *History* via Athenaeus, *Deipnosophistae* (4.152—Edelstein and Kidd F67); the stories of the Irish Finn and Amairgen can be found in many collections, including Patrick Ford's *The Celtic Poets* (1999,

4–37); Lucian's story of his visit to a Gaulish temple is found in his *Hercules* (1–6).

Reading: Unfortunately, no bardic poetry from ancient Gaul has survived the centuries, but medieval Irish and Welsh verse preserves many of the older Celtic themes. Patrick Ford's collection, mentioned previously, is an excellent source, as is Kenneth Jackson's *A Celtic Miscellany* (1971).

13. GODS

Epigraph: Julius Caesar, *Gallic War* (6.17).

Passages: Timaeus is quoted in Diodorus Siculus, *Geography* (4.56); the bird ritual of Eudoxus is from Aelian, *On the Nature of Animals* (17.19), while the Artemidorus passages are from Strabo, *Geography* (4.4.6); Caesar's complete description of the Gaulish gods, including father Dis, is from his *Gallic War* (6.17–18); the tale of the Gaulish seamen who transport departed souls is from Sozomen, *Ecclesiastical History* (1.5); the three cruel gods of Lucan are from his *Civil War* (1.444–446), while later commentary on the passage is collected in the medieval *Berne Scholia.*

Readings: The best introduction to the Gaulish gods is Proinsias Mac Cana's *Celtic Mythology* (1983)—in fact, I highly recommend the book to anyone seeking a firm grounding in ancient or medieval Celtic myth and legend. Miranda Green's short *Celtic Myths* (1995) is also a great start. One of the most useful tools for information on Gaulish gods and just about anything else in Celtic studies is Bernhard Maier's *Dictionary of Celtic Religion and Culture* (1997). An excellent work on the archaeology of Gaulish religion is Jean-Louis Brunaux's *The Celtic Gauls: Gods, Rites and Sanctuaries* (1988).

14. DRUIDS

Epigraph: Julius Caesar, *Gallic War* (6.14).

Passages: The first description by Posidonius is found in Strabo, *Geography* (4.4.4); the second is from Diodorus Siculus (5.31); the passage on criminal sacrifice is from Diodorus Siculus (5.32), while the augury involving human sacrifice is from the same author (5.31); Posidonius's fragment on Gaulish reincarnation is also preserved in Diodorus Siculus (5.28); Caesar's descriptions of the chief Druid, the annual meeting, the Druids' origins in Britain, education, and their teachings are all from his *Gallic War* (6.13–14), while his colorful passage on human sacrifice is from the same work (6.16); Cicero mentions the Druid Divitiacus in his *On Divination* (1.90); the gripping passage of Tacitus on the Roman slaughter at Anglesey is from his *Annals* (14.30); all three of Pliny's descriptions of Druidic rites are from his *Natural History*—mistletoe (16.24), the *selago* plant (24.103–104), and the serpent stone (29.52); the later Roman emperors who all meet a Druidess are from the *Historia Augusta:* Alexander Severus (*Alexander Severus* 59.5), Diocletian (*Numerianus* 14), and Aurelian (*Aurelianus* 43.4); the passage from Ausonius is found in his *Commemoratio* (4.7–10).

Readings: Bookstores are filled with works on the Druids—everything from Druidic history and archaeology to magic and astrology. My favorite for a solid introduction is Miranda Green's *The World of the Druids* (1997), which includes numerous archaeological photographs and also traces the development of modern Druidic movements. Stuart Piggott's *The Druids* (1975) is also very readable, as are *Druids* (1999) by Anne Ross and *The Life and Death of a Druid Prince* (1989) by Anne Ross and Don Robins. Nora Chadwick's *The Druids* (1966) is still well worth reading, along with T. D. Kendrick's *The Druids* (1966).

15. CONQUEST
Epigraph: Julius Caesar, *Gallic War* (1.26).

Passages: Caesar's description of his first invasion of Britain is found in his *Gallic War* (4.20–38), along with his second invasion (5.1–23); Vercingetorix describes his plan for fighting the Romans in the *Gallic War* (7.14), while the plan for eating the inhabitants of Alesia is found in the same book (7.77).

Reading: I recommend everyone go straight to the source for the conquest of Gaul and read Caesar's *Gallic War,* available in many good translations. Caesar was not only a brilliant general but also a clear and entertaining writer. We always have to keep in mind that he is putting forward his own side of the story, but he is more balanced and fair than many modern writers.

EPILOGUE: THE CELTIC HERITAGE
Epigraph: Tacitus, *Agricola* (24).

Passages: The Gaulish graffiti on spindle whorls are found in Wolfgang Meid's *Gaulish Inscriptions* (1992, 52–57); the passage on the Blasket Island poet is quoted from Tomás O'Crohan, *The Islandman* (1937; reprint 2000, 86—trans. Robin Flower).

Readings: One of the best short surveys of later Celtic history and literature is Bernhard Maier's *The Celts* (2003). The best translation of the Irish *Táin Bó Cuailnge* is by Thomas Kinsella (1969). My favorites among Blasket Island literature are Tomás O'Crohan's *The Islandman* (1937), Robin Flower's *The Western Island* (1944), and Peig Sayer's *An Old Woman's Reflections* (1962).

THERE'S NOTHING like seeing the art and archaeology of the ancient Celts up close at many of the excellent museums that feature such collections. I've listed a few of my favorites here, along with their websites. Most have displays of Celtic artifacts available for viewing online:

Austria: Kelten Museum, Pflegerplatz 5, Hallein
www.keltenmuseum.at

Czech Republic: Národní Muzeum, Václavské náměstí 68, Prague
www.nm.cz

Denmark: National Museum, Fredericksholms Kanal 12, Copenhagen
www.natmus.dk

England: British Museum, Great Russell Street, London
www.thebritishmuseum.ac.uk

France: Musée des Antiquités nationales, Château–Place Charles de Gaulle, Saint-Germain-en-Laye, France
www.musee-antiquitesnationales.fr

Germany: Württembergisches Landesmuseum Stuttgart, Schillerplatz 6, Stuttgart
www.landesmuseum-stuttgart.de

Ireland: National Museum of Ireland, Kildare Street, Dublin
www.museum.ie

Spain: Museo Arqueológico Nacional, Serrano, Madrid
www.man.es

Wales: National Museums and Galleries, Cathays Park, Cardiff
www.nmgw.ac.uk

INDEX

Achilles, 8, 28, 104, 162
Acichorius, 32, 34–35, 36
Adsagsona, 125
Aedui, 93–94, 97, 168, 177–78,
  179, 183
Aegosages, 42–43
Aeneid (Virgil), 66
Africa, 79
Agde, 88
Ager Gallicus (Gallic Lands), 59
Agricola, Gnaeus Julius, 191–92
Agricola (Tacitus), 189, 191–92
Alesia, 94, 98, 183–88, 192
Alexander Severus, Emperor of
  Rome, 172
Alexander the Great, 1–3, 30, 31,
  43, 46, 77, 90
Alexandria, 13, 67–68, 93
Alisanus, 156
Allobroges, 82
Alps, 3, 13, 19, 23, 56, 57, 58, 81
Amairgen, 140
Ambigatus, 58
Ambiorix, 181
Ammianus Marcellinus, 126
Anaximander, 14
Anglesey, 127, 170, 191
Anlúan, 131
Antigone (Sophocles), 112–13
Antiochus I Soter, King of Syria,
  41
Anyte, 40
Apamea, 7, 10–11
Aper, 172
Apollo, 3, 35–37, 145, 148–52,
  155
archaeology, 5, 18–25, 44–45,
  55–56, 57, 58, 71, 72,
  106–7, 113–14, 117, 123,
  132, 143, 149, 150, 151,
  160, 161, 166, 192
Argantokomaterekos, 66

Ariamnes, 132–33
Ariovistus, 177–78, 179
Aristotle, 1, 2, 13, 14, 27–28, 29,
  34, 82, 83, 84, 168, 176
armor, 105–6, 107, 108
Arruns, 58
Artemidorus of Ephesus, 147
Artemis, 45, 49–50
Arthur, King, 123, 155
Arverni, 93–94, 96, 138–39, 180,
  183
Asia Minor, 3, 13–14, 38, 39–40,
  43, 44, 46, 48, 78, 93, 102,
  144–45
Athena, 9, 84–85
Athenaeus, 130, 135
Athens, 7, 8, 9, 13, 23, 27, 52,
  55, 133–34
Atlantic Ocean, 21, 68, 70, 86–91,
  122, 145–46, 179
Attalus I, King of Pergamum, 41,
  42–43
Audacht Morainn, 96
Aurelian, Emperor of Rome, 172
Ausonius, 173

Bacchae (Euripides), 122
Bacchus, 122
bards, 66, 95, 98, 103, 110,
  138–43, 158, 163, 175,
  193–94
Basse-Yutz burial, 25
Belenus, 150–52
Belgae, 56, 94, 179, 181, 182,
  188
Belisama, 151
Bellovaci, 184
Bellovesus, 58–59
Beltane, 101
Bible, 69, 110–11
Bibracte, 94, 97–98, 178–79
Bithynians, 40, 43

as "Hierni," 21
historical references to, 21, 70,
    89, 147, 189, 192
language of, 194, 200
law texts of, 29, 117, 173–74
literature of, 70, 117–18,
    125–26, 131–32, 136, 137,
    139–40, 152, 166, 173–74,
    193, 194
medieval period of, 23, 29, 85,
    117–18, 131–32, 136, 137,
    139–40, 166, 173–74, 193
mythology of, 45, 75, 83–84,
    85, 117–18, 130–31,
    136–37, 140–41, 143,
    144–50, 151, 152–53, 155,
    173
poets of, 139–41, 193–94
religious traditions of, 24,
    117–18, 137, 140–41,
    146–47
as "sacred island," 70
trade of, 86, 89, 192–93
warfare in, 29, 103–4, 193
Irenaeus, Bishop of Lyon, 190
Irish Book of Invasions, 70, 152
Islandman, The (O'Crohan), 194

Jerome, Saint, 44
Jesus Christ, 41
Jews, 144, 152, 163
Julius Caesar, 173–88
    British campaigns of, 169–70,
        180–81
    Celtic gods described by, 75, 85,
        144, 148–53, 154
    Celtic women described by,
        119–21
    Druids described by, 44, 152,
        157, 163–68, 169, 173
    Gaul conquered by, 3, 48, 163,
        175–88
    military strategy of, 103–4,
        178–81
    political career of, 176–77, 187
    writings of, 144, 157, 175
Juno, 62–63
Jupiter, 8, 148, 149, 151, 154
Justin, 46, 78

Keltoi tribes, 3

Larzac tablet, 124–26
La Tène era, 23–25, 27, 30, 31,
    55, 56, 71, 85, 106–7, 115
Latin language, 20, 54, 61, 74, 81,
    189, 190, 192
Laws (Plato), 27
Leonorios, 39–40
Lepontii, 55–57, 72
Lewis and Clark expedition, 4, 92
Liguria, 53, 78, 79–81
Lindow Man, 161
livestock, 89–90, 99–101, 140,
    171
Livy, 57–58, 60, 61, 64, 111
Lleu, 75, 150
Llyn Cerrig Bach, 170
Loire River, 85, 88, 94, 121–23,
    148
Lucan, 153–54
Lucian, 141–42
Lucius Postumius, 65, 112
Lucretia, 57
Lucumo, 58
Lug, 75, 149–50
Lughnasadh, 75, 101, 150
Lugus, 75, 85, 101, 149–50, 151,
    152, 190
Lusitania, 68, 76
Lutorios, 39
Luvernius, 92, 96, 138–39
Lyon, 150, 190

Mabon, 154, 155
Macedonia, 1–3, 9–10, 31, 33
Macha, 155
magic, 124–26, 140, 146–47, 150,
    171–72, 190
Manlius, 48, 49
Maponus, 154–55
Marathon, Battle of, 9
Marius, Gaius, 55, 176
marriage, 29, 49–51, 82–84,
    118–21
Mars, 145, 148, 149, 151
Massalia, 78–91
    Celtic population of, 82–85, 86,
        93, 151
    as Greek colony, 21, 58, 78, 80,
        81–82, 84–87
    Posidonius's visit to, 53, 81,
        82, 92–93, 175